Civil Rights Memorials and the Geography of Memory

Nov. 3, 2008

For Matt.

Your research and perspectives on MLK streets helped make this book possible. I will always remember our adventures in Chapel Hill, High Point, and Grand Rapids.

Thanks,

Derek

Civil Rights Memorial by Maya Lin, Montgomery, Alabama.

Center Books on the American South
George F. Thompson, series founder and director

Civil Rights Memorials and the Geography of Memory

OWEN J. DWYER AND DEREK H. ALDERMAN

The Center for American Places at Columbia College Chicago

The Center for American Places at Columbia College Chicago
600 South Michigan Avenue
Chicago, Illinois 60605-1996, U.S.A.
www.americanplaces.org

Distributed by the University of Georgia Press
www.ugapress.uga.edu

16 15 14 13 12 11 10 09 08   1 2 3 4 5

Library of Congress Cataloging-in-Publication Data

Dwyer, Owen J.
    Civil rights memorials and the geography of memory / Owen J. Dwyer and Derek H. Alderman.
    -- 1st ed.
        p. cm. -- (Center books on the American South ; 11th v.)
    Includes bibliographical references.
    ISBN-13: 978-1-930066-71-7 (alk. paper)
    ISBN-10: 1-930066-71-6 (alk. paper)
    1. African Americans--Civil rights--Southern States--History--20th century. 2. Civil rights
    movements--Southern States--History--20th century. 3. Memorials--Political aspects--United
    States. 4. Memory--Social aspects--Southern States. 5. Memorials--Southern States. 6. Historic
    sites--Southern States. 7. Southern States--History, Local. 8. Southern States--Race relations--
    History--20th century. I. Alderman, Derek H. II. Title. III. Series.

    E185.61.D985 2008
    323.1196'073075--dc22

                        2008004830

ISBN-10: 1-930066-71-6 (hardcover)
ISBN-13: 978-1-930066-71-7 (hardcover)
ISBN-10: 1-930066-83-X (paperback)
ISBN-13: 978-1-930066-83-0 (paperback)

Frontispiece: Photograph by Owen J. Dwyer.

Contents

Prologue

Throughout their long career in the South, African Americans have waged an unceasing battle to secure places of their own in the midst of a hostile white society. These places range widely in terms of geographic extent. At one end of this spectrum lies the unrealized vision of a unified African continent; at the other are individual black bodies and the struggle to exercise free choice over their labor and love. In between are myriad elements of the built environment: free town and village, home and highway, field and school. These places, although often confined to the boundaries of a shared dream, testify to a tenacious will to thrive. The promise of these places has been anticipated, celebrated, and lamented in all manner of folk and popular media, often by those who sacrificed everything in their cause. Slowly, the histories of these people and places are being woven into the fabric of our collective memory and displayed at memorials around the nation.

It is out of admiration for this storied history of transgression and resistance that we have undertaken to write a book about the American Civil Rights Movement (hereafter referred to as the Movement). Within the span of a generation, cities and states across the country now commemorate the Movement. In order to understand this swelling tide, we examine the politics of producing civil rights memorials. To place these memorials in a broader context, we investigate the nation's existing landscape of communal allegiance found at courthouse lawns, in town squares, and along Main Street. Further, we explore the popular version of the Movement being presented in public space, paying close attention to which stories are remembered and which are forgotten. Finally, we offer some basic questions to serve as a method or guide for those exploring the geography of memory professionally or on their own.

As geographers interested in the relationship between place and culture, we have observed that the places around us reflect the priorities, tastes, and choices of those who produce them. In our unequal society, some people wield more place-shaping power than others. In turn, places exert their own subtle influence over society, broadcasting what is "known" to be important and trivial, honorable and corrupt, beautiful and repulsive.

Public space—in our case, the monuments, museums, parks, and streets dedicated to the Movement—is an especially potent site for transmitting notions of what is right and true, because it is authorized by the government on behalf of all citizens. For some, the imprint of state authority establishes a site's legitimacy. For others, government influence suggests co-option and inauthenticity. In either case, the state's role moves these sites out of the idiosyncratic and private (e.g., backyards, bumper stickers, and t-shirts) and into the public arena, a place where interests and ideologies compete for primacy.

Thus, geographers understand the relationship between society and space as reciprocal and reproductive. In *Civil Rights Memorials and the Geography of Memory*, we explore the politics of what our nation does and does not commemorate about the Movement and, importantly, *where* it does and does not do so. The legacy of Martin Luther King, Jr. is of central importance in these matters. For many, Dr. King embodies the Movement. Critically examining his contested legacy offers perspective on the Movement's collective memory and the ongoing struggle to claim space for it. Moreover, studying civil rights memorials—where they are located, what they honor, and what they forget—offers insights into the evolving verities of power and racism in American society. While the events that constitute the Movement's legacy are manifestly past, the act of identifying those events and interpreting their significance takes place in the present. These present-day interpretations will, in turn, affect the future.

Civil Rights Memorials and the Geography of Memory

Introduction

A Street Fight in Chattanooga, Tennessee

In January 1981, Reverend M. T. Billingsley petitioned the Chattanooga City Commission to name a street after slain civil rights leader Martin Luther King, Jr.[1] The timing of Rev. Billingsley's request, which came on behalf of the Ministers Union he helped lead, was freighted with great meaning. It took place just five days after King's birthday, January 16, which had not yet been made into a federal holiday, and less than a year after civil disturbances erupted in the city over the handing down of a controversial court verdict. An all-white jury acquitted two of three defendants arrested in connection with the Ku Klux Klan-related shooting of four black women. Ninth Street had been the location of the shooting, and, not coincidentally, it was also the road that black leaders sought to rename for King. Ninth Street had long served as the city's black business district, and it was the birthplace of blues legend Bessie Smith. According to Pastor Billingsley, Ninth Street was located "in the heart of Soulville."[2] In addition to his belief that renaming Ninth Street would lessen the black community's sense of alienation in the city, Billingsley felt that King's name would support redevelopment efforts in the area and "upgrade the social and physical aspects of the street."[3]

Several months of intense debate over the issue ensued. One of those opposed to the name change was T. A. Lupton, a white real estate developer who owned property on the western portion of the street. Lupton suggested that he might not be able to rent office space in a building with a King address because of the "racial overtones" it might create. He supported the renaming of East Ninth Street but not West Ninth Street, implying that the civil rights leader's memory would somehow be "out of place" there. He was quoted as saying: "West Ninth Street is not related to Dr. King. . . . [It] is no longer a solid black street. It is no longer a residential street or rundown business street. It is a top class business street that can play a great part in the future of Chattanooga."[4] The developer went so far as to suggest that he would abandon or drastically alter his construction plans in the event that West Ninth was renamed, thus throwing into jeopardy a federally funded redevelopment program for Chattanooga's downtown.

Lupton's opposition triggered a debate over the relative value of honoring Martin Luther King, Jr. with a street name. The real estate developer characterized the renaming proposal as a "symbolic gesture" and wondered how much good it would actually do for African Americans other than putting "another cloud" over his office project and his potential success in creating badly needed jobs in the city.[5] George Key, a local leader of the NAACP (National Association for the Advancement of Colored People), responded to Lupton's opposition by threatening to have federal money revoked for the redevelopment project if Ninth Street was not renamed.[6] Turning the tables, Key blamed the lack of economic development in Chattanooga on the racism displayed during the street-naming dispute. He was quoted as saying: "There's a lot of people, both tourists and business persons, who don't want to come to an area where there are racist attitudes and racial problems."[7]

Underlying the debate over renaming Ninth Street was what Gary Fine, a sociologist who studies commemoration, calls "reputational politics," a struggle to frame the meaning and importance of a historical reputation or legacy.[8] While Lupton implied that King's importance was limited to the black community, street-naming proponents asserted the cross-racial legitimacy of memorializing the civil rights leader. In making the argument for renaming all of Ninth Street, U.S. Representative Parren Mitchell, a former chairperson of the Congressional Black Caucus, explained: "All groups want monuments and symbols of their race. But with King, of course, it was more than a matter of race—it was the impact he had on this nation and this world."[9] African Americans in Chattanooga saw the city's opposition to the name change as a form of racism, expressed as a general disregard for a Nobel Peace Prize winner who died in pursuit of justice. Reverend Billingsley described Lupton's assertion that a King address would hamper business on Ninth Street as "a slap in the face of black people because Dr. Martin Luther King is one of the highly respected black people in America. You can take black out. . . . He's one of the highly respected people in America."[10]

Under pressure from Lupton and other opponents, Chattanooga's city commissioners refused to rename Ninth Street. As a compromise, the commission offered to establish a plaza in King's memory. Street-naming proponents quickly dismissed this alternative and responded by organizing a march along Ninth Street in late April 1981. Armed with ladders and singing the civil rights anthem, "We Shall Overcome," 300 protestors defiantly—albeit temporarily—renamed the street by pasting street signs and utility poles with green bumper stickers that read, "Dr. ML King Jr. Blvd."[11] At the march, black leaders characterized the street-naming struggle as an opportunity not only to celebrate King's achievements, but also to evaluate the degree to which society had fulfilled the Movement's goals, to "test whether 'equality' and 'justice' for all are valid statements, or whether they have no meaning at all."[12] On that same day, supporters assembled in a nearby park to hold a street dedication ceremony. One of the ministers presiding over the ceremony, Reverend Dr. Virgil Caldwell, captured the defiant nature of the event when he told the crowd, "Many people have taken it upon themselves to do what we must do to honor Dr. Martin Luther King … [w]hat the city fathers choose not to do."[13] Using tactics honed in the Movement itself, street-renaming proponents produced a memorial landscape in order to advance the politics of remembering King and the Movement.

After this protest and an emotional request from a coalition of white and black ministers, the Chattanooga City Commission reversed itself in July and agreed to rename all of Ninth Street for King as of January 1982.[14] Resistance to the proposal, however, continued. After initially opposing the proposed renaming, white city commissioner Paul Clark enthusiastically supported the effort to rename Ninth for King; soon thereafter he received numerous "hate-filled" phone messages from unidentified callers.[15] NAACP leaders would later encourage the boycott of a prominent Chattanooga hotel that had changed its mailing address from Ninth to a bordering street, presumably to avoid being identified with King. In the end, the street renaming did not stop Lupton, and he went forward with construction plans. The resulting office tower and its companion building, the corporate headquarters of the Krystal hamburger chain, however, do not have a King Street mailing address. Instead, a private drive was created, and the buildings reside on—presumably with no irony intended—Union Square.[16]

These events serve as a useful entry point for this book: Chattanooga is not the only city to have fought over how best to remember the Movement and its most widely recognized leader, Martin Luther King, Jr. Indeed, when petitioning local officials in Chattanooga to rename Ninth Street, several black leaders cited the fact that cities across the nation—

including the South—had already honored King with a street. Far from a single, isolated struggle, the street fight in Chattanooga became part of a growing movement to establish civil rights memorials across the United States, to build a new infrastructure of memory.

Less than a generation since its peak in the 1960s, the Movement is lauded in towns and cities whose names are synonymous with the hard-fought struggle against white supremacy: Topeka, Kansas; Little Rock, Arkansas; Oxford, Mississippi; Birmingham, Alabama; and Albany, Georgia. How did this come to be? That its memory is commemorated in places where shrill calls for "massive resistance" once rang out is fitting; in fact, today's efforts to remember the Movement can be thought of as yet another campaign to achieve racial equity.

In his study of the rise of multicultural consciousness, Joseph Tilden Rhea demonstrated that the growing movement to recognize the historical contributions of minorities involves a host of political, social, and economic dimensions.[17] That is to say, the trend toward celebrating America's multifarious heritage—a trend with its origins in the Movement—did not occur spontaneously, nor did it result from some inevitable force of history. Rather, the transformation of American public history's longstanding preoccupation with elite white men into something more representative of the nation's diversity is the result of concerted political efforts. Building upon the work of Gary Fine, we refer to the people who undertake to shape our understanding of the past as "memorial entrepreneurs": individuals, alone or in league with others, who endeavor to influence the meaning of social issues and debates about the past. Fine coined the term "reputational entrepreneur" to describe the role of social actors in shaping the reputation of specific historical figures.[18] Our notion of a memorial entrepreneur is slightly broader in that it recognizes the role of commemorative activism and agency in shaping not just historical reputations, but also the places produced for remembering the past. "Entrepreneur" derives from the French *entreprendre*, which refers to the undertaking of purposeful activity and is not necessarily limited to commercial enterprise. Working in a host of roles—as citizens, artists, authors, scholars, corporate managers, philanthropists, community organizers, and elected officials—memorial entrepreneurs engage in the risky, complicated, and sometimes contradictory process of commemorating the Movement. In the case of Chattanooga, the memorial entrepreneurs pushing for the renaming of Ninth Street recognized that public commemoration is part of democratic change and empowerment. After city leaders finally approved the renaming proposal, NAACP leader George Key concluded that the reversal shows that "black citizens are full citizens of Chattanooga and have a right to be considered in what goes on in [the city]."[19]

This book traces the spread of civil rights memorials across the United States, describes the version of the past they represent, and considers how audiences react to them. In complex ways, civil rights memorials simultaneously challenge and confirm the conventions that characterize commemoration in America. The arrival of the Movement's memorial legacy on the cultural landscape—the term that geographers use to describe the influence of people on the places around them—offers insight into its victories and shortcomings.

The Arrival of Civil Rights Memorials

While efforts to commemorate the Civil Rights Movement are a recent development, they signal the return of an earlier American tradition. Wilbur Zelinsky, an esteemed geographer who has long studied America's cultural landscape, described the practice of marking places—especially elements of the built environment, such as streets and buildings—to honor individuals and direct the public's attention to certain elements of the past.[20] For instance, Zelinsky found that twenty-five percent of counties and ten percent of streets in the United States are named after patriotic individuals or events. He observed, however, a dramatic decrease in nationalistic place-naming over the twentieth century, replaced by the commercial marketing of places via names with connotations of status and comfort. Events in Chattanooga illustrate this change in place-naming habits. Recall that real estate developer T. A. Lupton suggested the presence of King's name threatened his attempts to market property to potential tenants. Reverend Virgil Caldwell, the spokesman for a coalition of African–American leaders, countered that honoring King took precedence over economics: "We need a symbol. Dr. Martin Luther King symbolized progress for blacks, and we want a symbol for our young blacks. . . . Symbols are necessary to build hope, to build desire. And that is much more important than building mere buildings."[21]

While the gathering momentum to commemorate King and other civil rights leaders (such as Rosa Parks, Malcolm X, and Thurgood Marshall) represents a return to honoring inspirational heroes, it is significant that earlier patterns of commemoration in the United States were almost entirely devoted to lauding white men.[22] Civil rights memorials boldly challenge this pattern by representing the past and its heroes in more diverse terms, ones that specifically address experiences common to being black in America. In their book, *Presence of the Past*, Roy Rosenzweig and David Thelen found significant racial differences among Americans' attitudes toward the past.[23] To wit, African-American respondents were much more likely than whites to cite the assassination of Martin Luther King, Jr. as a historical event that affected them. They also found that blacks, more so than other Americans, fashion their historical consciousness around King's birthday and visiting memorials devoted to the struggle for civil rights.

Public commemoration of the Movement expanded during the last quarter of the twentieth century, propelled in part by the designation of King's birthday as a national holiday in 1983. Ironically, it is perhaps what the holiday could *not* offer African Americans that most inspired them to build civil rights memorials. Although the holiday has boosted efforts to commemorate King and the Movement, it is not universally observed by local governments and businesses. Unlike the holiday, which only occurs annually, a memorial or named place provides a physically permanent memorial that is present all the time and which requires local investment.

Not surprisingly, civil rights memorials are not uniformly distributed across the cultural landscape; they display a distinct geographic pattern. Perhaps the most widespread memorial to the Movement has been the naming of streets and other public places. As a stage for daily life, public places such as streets convey a quiet orthodoxy upon the Movement's legacy, marking it as part of the country's taken-for-granted historical consciousness. By 2003, at least 730 cities in the United States had named, or renamed, a street for King.[24] Although King streets are found throughout the nation, they are concentrated in the South. Georgia has the largest number, in part a reflection of the fact that so many civil rights organizations, campaigns, and leaders—including King himself—originated in the state.

Schools have also become popular sites for establishing the Movement's legacy. As of 2003, King's name had been attached to at least 122 public schools in thirty-five states and the District of Columbia.[25] Interestingly, the spatial pattern of King schools differs from

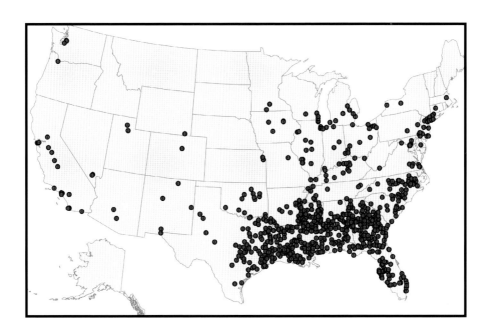

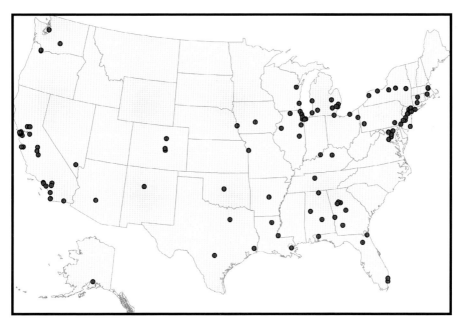

Top: places with a street named after Dr. Martin Luther King, Jr., 2003.

Bottom: places with a public school named after Dr. Martin Luther King, Jr., 2003.

Maps by Derek H. Alderman.

that of King streets: schools named for King are not concentrated in the South (with the exception of Georgia), but in predominantly African-American neighborhoods located in urban centers in California and the North. Geographer Roger Stump has speculated that the disparity may reflect the reluctance of white-dominated school districts to honor King in such an authoritatively public manner.[26] Indeed, in 1998, the Riverside, California, School Board voted to name a new, predominantly white high school after the civil rights leader, a decision that captured national media attention and sparked vehement protests from many white parents.[27] In a scene reminiscent of Lupton's objections in Chattanooga, opponents argued that their children might be perceived as being from a "black" school, thus hurting their children's chances of getting into good colleges. Political conflicts aside, geographic differences in school naming may also reflect instances in which African–American schools in the South were already named after black luminaries—including Washington, Carver, Wheatley, and Dunbar—bespeaking a historical consciousness that predates the post-Movement era. This much is certain: the topic deserves further study, inasmuch as the seemingly mundane matter of place naming provides scholars and activists alike an easily accessible entrepôt at which they may examine the voluminous baggage associated with American-style racial ideology.

Regional disparities characterize the spatial distribution of monuments and museums as well. Beginning with Maya Lin's *Civil Rights Memorial* (1989) in Montgomery, Alabama, no less than a dozen monuments and museums now commemorate the Movement. Clustered in the South, the most significant sites trace the history of the Movement from lunch counter sit-in protests in Greensboro, North Carolina, to the Lorraine Motel in Memphis, where Martin Luther King, Jr. was assassinated. Some of the memorials are quite humble: the monument dedicated to the four protestors shot by police in Orangeburg, South Carolina, is reserved in size and stature. Some memorials focus almost exclusively on local expressions of the Movement, such as the museums in Albany and Savannah, Georgia. Others tell a story that is national and international in scope, such as the King National Historic Site in Atlanta, Georgia. While the spatial distribution of these museums and monuments accords with the Movement's popular image as a Southern phenomenon, this regional disparity is significant and deserves a fuller explanation as it lends insight into forgotten aspects of the Movement.

As the nation's cultural landscape is reworked to reflect the experiences of African Americans, these new memorials sometimes clash with older, competing visions of the past. The result is a complex and often ironic landscape of collective memory. For instance, Atlanta's Martin Luther King, Jr. Drive ends at Oakland Cemetery, where *Gone with the Wind* author Margaret Mitchell and thousands of Confederate soldiers are buried. Further, King Drive was created from three previously named streets—Gordon Road, after Confederate General John B. Gordon; Hunter Street, after one of the largest slave owners in the area; and Mozley Drive, after a businessman who donated land for a park with the stipulation that it could be used only by whites.[28] Jefferson Davis Avenue intersects Martin Luther King Street in Selma. In Montgomery, Davis's namesake intersects Rosa Parks Avenue. Dixie Avenue crosses over King's namesake in Cartersville, Georgia. These intersecting streets raise an important issue: Can the Movement be honored in places that simultaneously pay tribute to the Confederacy? As the landscape is reshaped to represent more fully the South's past, the potential for an enriched collective memory grows. At a minimum, its public expression is being shorn of its racially exclusive, partisan character. At the same time, however, these intersections of memory also reflect the antagonistic nature of public commemoration in a region and nation where blacks and whites have long identified with, and sought to assert, the legitimacy of different visions of the past.[29] In other cases, the memorials reflect tensions from within the African-American community itself. Streets named after King and Malcolm X intersect in Dallas and Harlem. Their intersection visually alludes to each leader's related but distinct program for African-American empowerment.

More subtly, tensions within the Movement itself find their way onto the cultural landscape. Jackson, Mississippi's "Freedom Corner" is a case in point. A modest memorial marks the intersection of streets named for King and Medgar Evers. The inscription underneath King's image simply reads "I Have a Dream," while Evers's inscription reads "First NAACP Field Secretary in MS." The parallel commemoration of King and Evers overlooks the tension between the nation's largest civil rights organizations: King's Southern Christian Leadership Conference (SCLC) and the NAACP fought turf wars across the South for primacy in the Movement. More recently, the site has played host to a different kind of turf war occurring across the South. In 2001, a group led by a black city councilman burned a state flag at Freedom Corner as a protest against the Confederate battle emblem on Mississippi's official banner.[30]

The oft-strained relations between the Movement's local and national elements are also obscured in Selma, Alabama, where commemorative elements are interwoven. Situated along Selma's King Street is Browns Chapel A. M. E. Church. The church hosted mass meetings during the 1965 Voting Rights marches and is now the location of a monument dedicated to King. Ironically, local activists—most of whom remain nameless—resented King's influence over the voting rights struggle. The cultural landscape's tranquil pairing of the Movement's local and national elements is more seeming than real. Further, the presence of these hidden tensions attests to competing versions of the past. As geographer Brian Graham and his colleagues contend, the version of the past established by a memorial constitutes "a field of social conflict and tension, carrying differing and incompatible meanings simultaneously."[31] As described in the next section, a thorough analysis of civil rights memorials must look beneath the surface and study their symbols, reflect on their creation, and consider how audiences interpret them in order to understand the dynamic forces that shape them.

The Politics of Commemoration

From their inception, memorials are designed and planned, with all of the narrative choices and biases this entails, by those who have the time, resources, and public mandate to define the past. As art historian Kirk Savage has observed, memorials "do not arise as if by natural law to celebrate the deserving; they are built by people with sufficient power to marshal (or impose) public consent for their erection."[32] Groups across the political spectrum seek them out for rallies and photo opportunities. As part of the multi-million dollar heritage tourism industry, these memorials are often tailored to accommodate a broad range of interests. The role of memorials as tourist destinations and civic places links them to the city more broadly, bringing into question their place in urban redevelopment, real estate speculation, and plans for gentrification. Finally, the reliance of most memorials on state funding and corporate largesse makes them further susceptible to manipulation. The sum of these influences is that memorials are inherently political. They are also shaped by value-laden judgments and choices over what to remember and what to forget.

Memorials bear the imprint of society; in return, memorials exert a subtle social authority through their symbolic power and the audiences they attract. Memorials derive a portion of their authority by constituting a situation for everyday activity, accruing to themselves the naturalizing power of time and place. That memorials are commonly taken for granted does not render them irrelevant; the transformation from new to matter-of-fact suggests that a memorial's message enjoys a measure of orthodoxy. This orthodoxy is a form of power—the power of the norm—as a particular interpretation of the past becomes granted, assumed. The subtle, soft power of memorials is on display in the case of naming streets after historical figures. Street naming allows a certain vision of the past to be incorporated into the everyday settings and activities of the city, structuring the very language that people use.[33] The presence of memorials sends the message that this is History, properly commemorated and ready to edify all who walk within view.

Memorials wield further social influence due to the common impression that they are impartial records of the past. In the case of monuments and museums, their location in public space, weighty presence, and the enormous amounts of financial and political capital such installations require imbue them with an air of authority and permanence. Relative to personal and corporate media (such as television, books, films, and music), they appear to be a lasting and official record of the past, above political bias and worthy of admiration. Further, their apparent permanence suggests the possibility of anchoring a fleeting moment in time to an immovable place. Composed of seemingly elemental substances—water, stone, and metal—memorials cultivate the appearance that the true, authentic past is and will remain within reach.

The designers of civil rights memorials reinforce the sense of being immersed in the past with realistic statuary, informative plaques, and documentary photos. Apparently, the goal is to give visitors the sense of witnessing the past. In contrast to much contemporary art—which can emphasize abstract expressionism and self-scrutiny at the expense of figural realism—civil rights memorials are unabashedly referential. They seek to teach visitors about the past, not the process through which the past has come to be known. With few exceptions, civil rights memorials do not call attention to ambiguous motives, painful doubts, or alternative interpretations; the point is to offer public testimony to what happened, to whom, and where. Consider Maya Lin's striking memorial in Montgomery, with its select names of those who died in the Movement; or the literalism of statues and streets dedicated to Martin Luther King, Jr.; or the emphasis more generally on plaques and markers to highlight places in what has become the conventionally historic manner. Overall, these memorials are intended to act as memory aids: they seek to make tangible the past itself, not to promote insights into how our knowledge of the past is shaped by the living.

Ironically, memorials often disappoint those who make them: rather than establishing an authoritative recounting of the past, they commonly open new debates over its meaning and significance. By virtue of their *gravitas*—both literal and figurative—memorials seemingly promise to place the past beyond the vagaries of reinterpretation. Yet, a memorial cannot speak for itself. It relies on an audience's interpretation, and its meaning can change accordingly. Even the most seemingly straightforward, explicit memorial—and the event it represents—can be reinterpreted as a result of changes in time and place.

Thus, memorials are inviting targets for activists who see in them the opportunity to generate political capital. The contrast between a monument's stark visibility and tremulous meanings renders it vulnerable to attack. The once-celebrated Liberty Monument in New Orleans offers a case in point. Erected in 1891 to commemorate the White League, a paramilitary organization that spearheaded the drive to disenfranchise African Americans in Reconstruction-era Louisiana, the Liberty Monument was long a fixture along Canal Street, the city's main thoroughfare. In the Movement's wake, a succession of African-American mayors and city councils lobbied against its presence to no avail. Then, in 1989, under the pretense of street repairs, it was removed and deposited in a city warehouse. With the street repairs completed, an odd coalition of white supremacists and historic preservationists began lobbying for the monument to be reinstalled. Counter-protestors—many of them civil rights activists—argued that the monument celebrated an illegal action and, moreover, was an offense to the city's black majority. A federal court ruled on the matter, stating that the monument must be reerected but not necessarily at the same location. Obligingly, the city reinstalled the monument at a new, less prominent location—largely hidden on an unremarkable parcel between a parking lot, the aquarium, and a light-rail line. Importantly, the rededicated monument included a new plaque, one that contradicts the spirit of the monument's original inscription by praising those who died fighting the White League. James Loewen, a veteran observer of the nation's racial politics, noted that the controversy engendered by the Liberty Monument acted as "something of a barometer showing the relative power of blacks and whites in this part of America, and the importance each group places on control of the landscape."[34]

Despite their realism and the hopes of those who finance and make them, memorials cannot be imbued with an essential, enduring meaning. The fracas over the Liberty Monument demonstrated that, insofar as a memorial claims to present *the* authoritative version of the past, it furnishes different audiences with the raw material for a new round of criticism regarding what is "true" or "real." Witness the comments of Reverend Avery Alexander, a civil rights activist from New Orleans, who campaigned against the Liberty Monument. In reference to it, he said:

> [The Liberty Monument] is like the Confederate flag. It's something
> that people who want to see a return to the old days, a return to
> the Confederacy, can rally around. But every time they do, they are
> reminding us of the way things once were, of their love for those old,
> old days.[35]

The White League presumably neither envisioned that its monument would become a rallying point for civil rights activists, nor could they have foreseen its transformation into an anti-monument to white supremacy. Nevertheless, memorials are vulnerable to radical reinterpretation as their moorings shift in the swirling pools of time and place. It will be interesting to see if the memorial undergoes further reinterpretation in the wake of Hurricane Katrina and the changing demographics of the city. While memorials exude a sense of longevity and stability, their meanings are not impervious to change. Beneath the appearance of historical consensus and stability, memorials—and, by implication, the meaning and significance of the events they represent—are the product of, and conduit for, ongoing debate. In this sense, memorials do not simply record the past; by providing a means of articulation, memorials are implicated in the production of the past itself. Exploring the manner in which memorials are laden with interests, both served and denied, is the purpose of the chapters that follow.

The Geography of Memory

Establishing a civil rights memorial is not only a struggle over history, but also a matter of geography. While it is true that every past event has a location associated with it, the relationship between commemoration and geography is more complicated than temporal and spatial coordinates. The question of *where* the past should be commemorated is frequently a contentious matter. These arguments need not be limited to questions regarding the geographical accuracy of the historic record. Commonly, they have more to do with questions of contemporary geography than the past. Where an event is commemorated—and, conversely, where it is not commemorated—affects how it is remembered. Again, events in Chattanooga are instructive. The street-renaming controversy highlighted the importance that both proponents and opponents attached to putting memory in its proper place. Whereas a white real estate developer and his supporters sought to position Ninth Street as a rising commercial address, the street was also closely associated with the city's once-thriving black business district and a shocking incident of racial violence. The debate was not restricted to King's legacy; it involved the meaning of the street as well.

With place and memory inextricably linked, each side attempted to articulate a compelling image for the street. In effect, both parties recognized that a memorial's location dramatically influences its meaning and vice versa. Opponents of the street-renaming proposal argued that King's significance was limited to the city's African-American community and, as a result, only a small portion of Ninth Street should be renamed. Their proposal to divide the street suggested that King's memory did not belong outside the traditional bounds of the city's black community; to do otherwise, they held, would be inappropriately sectarian for a public space and might subsequently harm the area's economic redevelopment. Proponents countered that King's message of the "Beloved Community" was relevant to whites as well as blacks. Accordingly, an expansive vision of brotherhood and solidarity deserved to be attached to all of Ninth Street, including the western portion, where white-led economic redevelopment was taking place. Dividing Ninth Street and renaming the small portion associated with African Americans, they argued, would be tantamount to segregating King's memory. In the end, proponents carried the day but not before confronting the important role that geography plays in commemorating the Civil Rights Movement.

Geographers study where things are located, why they are there, and how their presence affects the world around them. These questions form the basis of the spatial perspective used to investigate a host of topics, including commemoration. When studying a memorial, geographers pay special attention to its site and situation. A memorial's site refers to the specific condition of its placement. A description of a memorial's site would note such elements as its visibility, accessibility, symbolic elements, and adjacency to other parts of the landscape. In contrast, a memorial's situation is examined more broadly in relation to the rest of the city or countryside. Relevant issues here include its location vis-à-vis the area's mosaic of race-, gender-, and class-based patterns; its proximity to power-filled sites, such as the central business district or other memorials; and the flow pattern of tourists and visitors and, just as importantly, those who do not visit.

Geographers use the term "cultural landscape" to encompass their interest in explaining the intricacies of the tangible, visible scene of site and situation. Thus, when geographers study memorials as cultural landscapes they consider not only a memorial's content and form, but also its placement and relative location. This emphasis on studying memorials as elements in a broader cultural landscape—one that is the product of struggle and compromise—is particularly important in the context of civil rights memorials. Typically, Movement activists challenged the legitimacy of racial boundaries, many of which were inscribed in laws and habits that admonished individuals to "know their place." For latter-day civil rights activists, establishing memorials that transcend these boundaries—boundaries related to racist notions of whose history belongs where—provides a litmus test of how far society has progressed toward the goal of racial equity and justice. For instance, the demand that all of Chattanooga's Ninth Street be renamed embodied a bid to ensure that the spatial extent—the scale—of King's legacy transcended the city's racial boundaries. In doing so, organizers challenged the tradition of the racial segregation of memory. Geographers study memorials in their spatial context because a memorial's "place" goes beyond mere coordinates to simultaneously reflect and influence society.[36]

The condition of memorials in the cultural landscape influences what is remembered and forgotten. In *Presence of the Past*, Rosenzweig and Thelen presented evidence that Americans, despite being bored with studying history in school, "make the past part of their everyday routines and turn to it as a way of grappling with profound questions about how to live."[37] These scholars found that the cultural landscape plays a central role in how the public connects with, uses, and learns from the past. Fifty-seven percent of the almost 1,500 people interviewed by Rosenzweig and Thelen said they had visited a history museum or historic site within the past twelve months. Important books by James Loewen and Townsend Davis make a similar point: cultural landscapes are important to the process of remembering, inasmuch as assigning history a place gives it a tangible, lasting presence—albeit with a meaning that can shift and slip unexpectedly.[38] After observing and studying many of America's memorials, cultural geographer Kenneth Foote argues that "[t]he physical durability of landscape permits it to carry meaning into the future so as to help sustain memory and cultural traditions."[39] Birmingham, Alabama's Kelly Ingram Park is one such place that has been explicitly reworked in order to define the Movement's collective memory.[40]

Redesigned and rededicated as "A Place of Revolution and Reconciliation" in 1992 by Richard Arrington, the city's first African-American mayor, Kelly Ingram Park commemorates the protests that desegregated the city. The project's designers sought to remind future generations that no meaningful reconciliation in Birmingham could be achieved between the races without a revolution in their relationship—no justice, no peace. Likewise, the gains of the revolution would be pyrrhic if the result was an embittered division, a point not lost on perceptive observers of a Birmingham whose schools, residences, and churches are nearly as segregated today as they were a half century ago, albeit this time without the law's backing. Using the park as a setting for these twinned themes—revolution and reconciliation—did not come about by chance; the park's history as a Movement-era battlefield lent itself to the connection.

As was the case in Chattanooga, place and memory are inseparable at Kelly Ingram Park. At one time segregated for the use of whites only, the park is closely associated with the Movement. It was the site at which Bull Conner's police attacked protesters—many of them children—with dogs and fire hoses in 1963. Civil rights workers dubbed the city "Bombingham" due to the impunity with which the Ku Klux Klan planted dynamite throughout the black community. In the wake of the successful protests in Birmingham, the then-shaky coalition planning the March on Washington gathered strength and, in turn, spurred passage of the landmark Civil Rights Act of 1964. And, finally, several months after the successful protests, the Klan dynamited nearby Sixteenth Street Baptist Church, killing four girls preparing for worship. Sitting adjacent to the park and astride the boundary between white and black Birmingham, the church was attacked for allowing protesters to use its cavernous sanctuary as a meeting place and staging area. In the geography of the Movement, Kelly Ingram Park is a wellspring, a central place from which a concentrated force of sorrow, rage, and resolve spread out across the land.

Today, tens of thousands of memorial pilgrims seek out the park, the restored Sixteenth Street Baptist Church, and the Birmingham Civil Rights Institute. Not unlike a book or other work of art, the authors of Birmingham's memorial landscape intended it to be read and interpreted. The legibility of a place is another aspect of the relationship between geography and memory: landscapes can be reworked either to clarify or obscure the events associated with them. For instance, Kelly Ingram Park offers a public primer in the Movement's fundamental tactic: the orchestrated confrontation between the innocence of nonviolent protest and the brutal response of unveiled white supremacy. Paved with slabs of flinty black slate, a narrow walkway circumscribes the park; it is impossible to enter the park's contemplative center without confronting the menacingly large sculptures that straddle the walkway. The close, visceral presence of the statuary along the path— not abstract shapes but frighteningly realistic dogs and water cannons—offers a poignant study in opposites. The hulking jail and lunging dogs are opposed by nothing more than the budding courage of children. Contrary to the conventional presentation of American history, Kelly Ingram Park has been reshaped in order to witness the contributions of African Americans. That a commemorative statuary park occupies the ground of a pivotal moment in the Civil Rights Movement is a telling sign of how the moment was resolved.

That said, the park's portrait of the Movement is complicated. As with any work of art, cultural landscapes bear a host of interpretations. Dell Upton, a keen observer of America's built environment, has explained that what appears on the surface to be a single, powerful testimony to the Movement yields, upon closer inspection, a complex meditation on the spectrum of political traditions within black Birmingham.[41] These contrasting approaches to social justice reflected class and denominational differences, as well as judgments about the efficacy of protest vis-à-vis economic empowerment. Upton observed that the character of the park's diagonal paths mirror these differences. Raymond Kasky's statue of three kneeling ministers anchors the northwest-southeast axis that faces the city's white business district. The faithful witness of the ministers, with their massed presence and purposeful countenances, serves as a reminder of the potent mix of prayer and protest that confronted the white power structure when it sought to squash the Movement. Behind the ministers rise Sixteenth Street Baptist Church and a statue of Dr. King. The axis created by the ministers and the church simultaneously conveys a powerful, albeit nonviolent, summons to heed the dictates of American democracy.

The park's other axis speaks to a different strategy for making good on America's promise. Anchored by four charcoal-gray stelae, this corner of the park faces the Fourth Avenue business district, historically the center of Birmingham's African-American business community. Inscribed with a name, a brief testimony, and a bronze low-relief profile, each stela recounts the efforts of a black professional to serve Birmingham's African-American community. Fourth Avenue—which, today, seeks to revivify itself as an arts and entertainment district—is dominated by the architectural remains of A. G. Gaston's commercial empire. A life-long Alabamian, Gaston—and, more generally, Birmingham's black commercial and religious elite—was critical of the Movement's tactics of direct action. A firm critic of white supremacy, Gaston nevertheless hewed to Booker T. Washington's advice to strive for economic power within the confines of segregation. The subdued character of the stelae reflects Washington's approach toward affecting positive change in the African-American community—one that eschewed political confrontation and looked to accommodate multiple interests through quiet negotiations and the accumulation of wealth.

Fourth Avenue's current struggle to reclaim some portion of its prior glory testifies to the limitations of nonviolent political protest vis-à-vis Gaston's pragmatic emphasis on "green" power. Perversely, black business districts, such as Birmingham's, went into accelerated decline in the wake of desegregation. Black businesses collapsed under the weight of intense competition and shifting tastes as their once-captive audience exercised its freedom to shop elsewhere. While King's brand of direct action secured political and social gains, it had the bitterly ironic repercussion of undoing the conditions that allowed black business districts to thrive. Further, the economic injustices that working-class blacks continue to suffer have proved stubbornly resistant to the method. Pointing as it does toward a blighted landscape, this axis undermines Kelly Ingram Park's declaration of victory and ringing endorsement of the strategy of nonviolent protest.

Upton's observation that two different prescriptions for progress cross paths at Kelly Ingram Park—revolution and reconciliation—illustrates the manner in which memorials bear the impress of those who create them. Kelly Ingram Park's layout and content reflect differing ideas about how best to promote civil rights. Thus, memorials carry many messages, messages that can only be made legible by appreciating their geographic situation. Furthermore, anchoring a particular version of the past in the landscape is a time-honored strategy for cultivating cultural capital. Observing how the streets in his Harlem neighborhood had been renamed after prominent figures in African-American history, Melvin Dixon pointed to this fact: "What you may gather from these names and places is a sense of changes within history…the fact that people have taken charge of their lives and their identity as African Americans. Not only do these names celebrate and commemorate great figures in black culture, they provoke our active participation in that history. What was important yesterday becomes a landmark today."[42]

Dixon's poignant remark testifies to the power of mixing history and geography; it also inspires a number of questions about the conditions under which they meet. For instance, if commemoration is an act of power, then we must ask a series of questions. How do landmarks come to be? Which stories do they embrace and which ones are rejected? Why is a landmark placed *here* and not *there*? And, finally, how do people—visitors, activists, passersby—interact with memorials?

The stories that lie behind these places of commemoration reflect the will to define collective memory. Once the memorials are set in place, however, audiences often interpret them in ways their creators never intended. Because memorials can be interpreted in multiple, sometimes conflicting ways, they do more than simply reflect ideas and secure them to the ground; they extend these ideas into the world and, in so doing, hold them up for emulation or criticism. In effect, a memorial functions as a negotiating table or arena over which to parlay the future in terms of the past. Tomorrow's civil rights strategies will be influenced by a host of factors, among them the Movement's legacy on the cultural landscape. In this sense, the future can, in part, be traced back to what is remembered and forgotten on the cultural landscape. Dixon's comments about Harlem highlight a crucial point: the stakes associated with commemoration are high, and making sense of memorials requires background knowledge and interpretive techniques. This book is offered as an aid in this complex task.

What to Expect from This Book

Your journey into the Movement's legacy may take you to dozens of sites across the South. Along the way, you will have the opportunity to tour museums, view public landmarks, and walk historic streets. You may talk with curators, historians, shop owners, and activists. Experiencing the memorial landscape firsthand conveys the Movement's history more intensely than reading a book or viewing a documentary. For instance, if you make the trip to the National Civil Rights Museum in Memphis, you will have the chance to climb aboard a 1950s-era bus. By today's standards, the coach is cramped, perhaps uncomfortably intimate. Taking a seat, a white bus driver curtly tells you to move to the back of the bus. As his threats escalate, the space inside the bus intensifies; quite literally, there is nowhere to hide. Surrounded by strangers, confronted by authority, you may realize, maybe for the first time, just how easy it would have been to keep your head down, to mind your own business, to look the other way. Likewise, the experience may grant you a richer appreciation for the enormous courage it would take to break the rules in order to uphold a higher law.

Geographers are particularly interested in the way the Movement's history is being written on and through the cultural landscape. Conveyed through a mosaic of objects and places—buses, parks, lunch counters, street corners, and motel balconies—the Movement leaves a powerful impression on those who study it. These impressions have been carefully anticipated and cultivated by the designers of civil rights memorials. As we made our own journeys to these sites, the intensity of the cultural landscape left us awed by the uncommon courage and staggering sacrifices that made the civil rights revolution possible. It also made us aware that the Movement is far from concluded. For many, the Movement's promise has yet to be realized fully. Despite its numerous victories—legislative, electoral, economic, and social—the struggle to secure a just and equitable future for all Americans continues. The retelling of the Movement's history is part of this ongoing effort; in effect, commemorating the Movement is but the latest battle in the ongoing campaign for civil rights.[43] Written into the landscape, different versions of the Movement's past are vying for attention. These differences interested us. The groups responsible for commemorating civil rights history, with their complex—some might say contradictory—coalitions captured our attention as well. We also noticed the manner in which these sites are taking on a life of their own as places to conduct a wide array of activities, ranging from weighty protests to simple picnics. We became aware that there are important stories to be told about the historical sites, stories that are tightly bound to the places around them. Our aim in this book is to investigate these landscapes and consider their significance.

In examining civil rights memorials and the interests associated with them, we will, out of necessity, recount incidents from the Movement. Our main focus, however, is not retelling the past but rather investigating the manner in which the past is being portrayed selectively on and through the cultural landscape. Several guides to civil rights history do an excellent job of thoughtfully ushering visitors from site to site.[44] In addition, a growing body of scholarship probes the relationship between commemoration, society, and the cultural landscape.[45] It is required reading for any serious student of collective memory and the manufacture of consent.

This book differs from these indispensable guides and thoughtful studies in its exclusive focus on the stories and struggles associated with the way Americans are creating places to commemorate the Movement. Each chapter is organized around a central question, the answers to which are crucial for making sense of the Movement's legacy in contemporary America.

In Chapter One, we take stock of the stories that are included and excluded from civil rights memorials. No memorial, however ambitious and well-funded, can include all of the stories associated with an event or person. That said, interpreting a memorial in terms of what is present and absent offers a method for intuiting what its creators believed was essential about the Movement and, by implication, what they believed was manifestly not.

In Chapter Two, we investigate the politics and economics associated with the creation of two representative types of civil rights memorials: civil rights museums and Martin Luther King, Jr. streets. To subject such hallowed ground to the vulgar metric of dollars and influence may seem inadmissibly rude. That said, how many of us will undertake so bold a gambit as to shape collective memory, to cast its outline in stone, earth, and steel? The sheer magnitude of the task, and its attendant ambition, is daunting. Presenting our analysis in terms of economic and political interest offers a stratagem for rendering more familiar the terrific forces that memorial entrepreneurs dare to wield.

In Chapter Three, we scrutinize the uneven spatial distribution of civil rights memorials. As alluded to in this introduction, memorials do not always appear where we would expect them. Careful study of the relative location of these places offers insights into the ambitions that underpin them, disclosing along the way commitments that might otherwise go unnoticed if their arrangement in public space was ignored.

Finally, in the Conclusion, we offer three principles and thirty questions that may enhance the experience of visiting and interpreting civil rights memorials. Our intention is to promote an active engagement with places of collective memory, rather than passively accepting them. In the spirit of the Movement itself, we offer these principles and the questions that accompany them as a way to honor the past by nurturing the future. The following photographic gallery presents a visual display of our thesis.

Gallery

PHOTOGRAPHS BY OWEN J. DWYER
except as otherwise noted

1. Inscription outside the Lincoln Memorial, Washington, D.C.

The site of Reverend Martin Luther King, Jr.'s memorable address to the nation on August 28, 1963, is honored in this simple, but unforgettable way. The understatement of fact becomes self-evident to all who remember Dr. King's inspirational words in this consecrated place.

2. Protestors on Ninth Street, Chattanooga, Tennessee.

Faced with City Council's unwillingness to rename all of Ninth Street in honor of Martin Luther King, Jr., ladder-bearing marchers took matters into their own hands. Underlying the renaming debate was the knotty question of the scale at which King's legacy would be commemorated. City Council's proposal to rename the eastern and largely black portion of Ninth Street implied that King's importance was limited to the African-American community. Proponents of renaming all of Ninth Street felt that King's message should be expansive and not limited to the boundaries of a specific neighborhood. In making the argument for renaming all of Ninth Street, U.S. Representative Parren Mitchell explained: "All groups want monuments and symbols of their race. But with King, of course, it was more than a matter of race—it was the impact he had on this nation and this world." The street-renaming controversy highlighted the importance that both proponents and opponents attached to putting memory in its proper place. (Photograph reprinted with the permission of the Chattanooga Regional History Museum.)

3. Renaming Ninth Street, Chattanooga, Tennessee.

In front of crowds cheering "hallelujah," the Reverend M. T. Billingsley pasted street signs and utility poles with bumper stickers that read, "Dr. ML King Jr. Blvd." Afterward, supporters assembled in nearby Miller Park to hold a dedication ceremony. One of the ministers presiding over the ceremony, Reverend Dr. Virgil Caldwell, captured the defiant nature of the event when he told the crowd, "Many people have taken it upon themselves to do what we must do to honor Dr. Martin Luther King . . . [w]hat the city fathers choose not to do." Using tactics honed in the Movement itself, street-renaming proponents produced a memorial landscape in order to advance the "reputational politics" of remembering King and the Movement. In doing so, they underscored art historian Kirk Savage's observation (see note 32 on p. 109) that memorials "do not arise as if by natural law to celebrate the deserving; they are built by people with sufficient power to marshal (or impose) public consent for their erection." (Photograph reprinted with the permission of the Chattanooga Regional History Museum.)

4. East 5th Street and King Drive, Greenville, North Carolina.

West 5th Street became Martin Luther King, Jr. Drive in 1999. Originally, African-American leaders wanted all of 5th Street renamed—not just part of it—but residents and business owners on the eastern end strongly opposed the proposal. King's namesake marks an area that is predominantly black, whereas East 5th is mostly white. More recent attempts to rename all of 5th Street have failed, leading to deep frustration within the city's African-American community. In the words of one black elected official, "The accomplishments of Dr. King were important to all Americans. A whole man deserves a whole street!" Across the nation, street-naming opponents consistently impose strict spatial limits on such proposals, in effect seeking to limit King's memorial to black areas. The sad irony is that, while King challenged segregation, his legacy is often fixed at a scale that reinforces contemporary racial boundaries. Scale, according to geographer Neil Smith, has a "double-edged nature": it can both constrain the visibility of causes and enlarge them. In the time since this photograph was taken, another call to honor King down the rest of 5th Street emerged, causing several months of intense public debate. Seeking to settle what they saw as a "divisive" issue, white municipal leaders voted in February 2007 to rename the city's bypass for King and ordered that the existing Martin Luther King Jr. Drive revert back to West 5th Street. In response, African Americans in Greenville must now bear the expense and inconvenience of changing their address to ensure, in effect, that white property owners on East 5th Street would not have to do so. (Photograph by Derek H. Alderman.)

5. Martin Luther King, Jr. Parkway, Lafayette, Louisiana.

The most vocal opponents to naming streets after Martin Luther King, Jr. are often business and property owners, who cite the cost and inconvenience of a change in address. This resistance has led some cities to dedicate portions of streets to civil rights leaders rather than carry out a full renaming. This was the case in 2007, when the city-parish council of Lafayette, Louisiana, dedicated Willow Street to Dr. King. Lafayette already had a street named for the civil rights leader, but two African-American members of the council argued that the road was not prominent enough. The debate became so heated that protests were carried out in front of City Hall, and one black councilman was arrested and fined for defacing public property after he carved "Dr. Martin Luther King Jr." into his council desk. The dedication of Willow Street was proposed by Lafayette's mayor as a political compromise. Simply attaching honorary signs to the road, however, is not the same as an address change: King's name is less likely to appear on city maps, business advertisements, phone books, and travel directions. Some activists argue that dedicating streets, while a highly visible form of commemoration, does not carry the same dignity as renaming and that it still does not require the larger white community to interact with, and invest personally in, memorials to the Movement. Indeed, even when the cost of an address change has not been an issue, white citizens in some cities have opposed having honorary King signs placed in their neighborhoods in an attempt to protect racial boundaries. (Photograph by Leslie Westbrook; reprinted with the permission of *The Daily Advertiser*.)

6. Intersection of Jefferson Davis Avenue and Martin Luther King, Jr. Street, Selma, Alabama.

As the South's cultural landscape is reworked to include the experiences of African Americans, new memorials sometimes clash with older, competing visions of the past. For instance, Atlanta's Martin Luther King, Jr. Drive ends at Oakland Cemetery, the final resting place for *Gone with the Wind* author Margaret Mitchell and thousands of Confederate soldiers. Sites such as these intersecting streets in Selma raise a contentious question: To what extent can the Movement be honored in places that simultaneously pay tribute to the Confederacy? The arrival of African-American-themed memorials on the grounds of state capitols across the South (see Figure 41) seemingly answers the question in the affirmative: historically twinned, their memory will be preserved in geographic proximity. As the landscape is reshaped to represent more fully the region's past, the potential for an enriched collective memory grows. At a minimum, its public expression is being shorn of its racially exclusive, partisan character.

7. Ralph Mark Gilbert Civil Rights Museum, Savannah, Georgia.

Visitors armed with some background knowledge of the Movement are in a position to reflect on the memorial landscape's ironies. In Savannah, Georgia, Dr. King's namesake street plays host to the Ralph Mark Gilbert Civil Rights Museum, named after the "father" of the city's civil rights struggle. During the civil rights demonstrations of the 1960s, black leaders in Savannah tried to bar Martin Luther King, Jr. from preaching in the city. They feared that his presence might antagonize local authorities, disrupt an already successful protest movement, and perhaps steal some of their thunder. The cultural landscape's tranquil pairing of the Movement's local and national elements is more seeming than real. The presence of these hidden tensions attests to competing versions of the past. Also, neighborhood conditions—such as underutilized lots on either side of the museum pictured here—characterize many civil rights memorials and speak to the current challenges and conditions that African Americans face in the wake of so-called "urban renewal" and desegregation. (Photograph reprinted with the permission of the *Savannah Morning News*.)

8. Jefferson Davis Monument on the grounds of the capitol, Montgomery, Alabama.

As the birthplace of two intertwined American revolutions, the Civil War and the Civil Rights Movement, Montgomery's cultural landscape—the term that geographers use to describe the reciprocal influence of people and places—is extraordinarily rich. Two of its most poignant sites of collective memory are pictured here and in Figure 9. No more than a city block from the statue of Jefferson Davis is the church from which Martin Luther King, Jr., led the year-long boycott that desegregated the city's buses in 1956. The uncanny proximity of the two sites bespeaks the complexity of Montgomery's cultural landscape: one icon fought to leave the United States while the other gave his life to be included fully in it. Now they are both enshrined in the city's collective memory. How are we to understand this scene?

9. Dexter Avenue King Memorial Baptist Church, Montgomery, Alabama.

Peirce F. Lewis, the eminent cultural geographer, suggests that we interpret landscapes, such as Montgomery's, as one would a book: "Our human landscape," he wrote in 1979 (see note 2 on p. 122), "is our unwitting autobiography, reflecting our tastes, our values, our aspirations, and even our fears, in tangible, visible form." Lewis developed this line of reasoning—landscape-as-text—in order to decode the intricacies of cultural artifacts. Above all, Lewis encouraged close inspection of landscapes—embodied in thoughtful preparation before a trip, careful observation throughout, and critical inquiry in its wake—as an alternative to accepting memorials at face value. Close inspection of the Lewisian sort can transform passive heritage tourism into an active engagement with the politics of memory.

10. Historic marker, Montgomery, Alabama.

Rosa Parks died in 2005, a month shy of the fiftieth anniversary of what was, in 1955, a bitterly contested matter. Within her lifetime, she witnessed the installation of an official marker at the point where she politely resisted the mundane trappings of life in a white supremacist society. The relative speed with which her story—albeit narrowly interpreted as a matter of true grit, seating preference, and public accommodation—was enshrined on the cultural landscape is a tangible sign of the Movement's social authority, of its assumed "common sense" status. As is the case with streets named after the Movement's luminaries, historical markers exhibit the subtle, soft power of everyday memorials to incorporate a vision of the past into common settings. The result is a place that helps to establish a version of the past as "History." Parks's legacy is not without irony: the bus stop that stood at this spot was replaced long ago by parking spaces. The private car has conclusively settled the issue of who would sit next to whom on the bus: public transit riders in Montgomery today are almost exclusively black.

11. Rosa Parks Library and Museum, Troy State University, Montgomery, Alabama.

Troy State's campus offers a thoroughly contextual treatment of Rosa Parks's career, a welcome departure from the relatively shallow treatment she typically receives elsewhere on the memorial landscape. For instance, photographs in the library depict Parks's participation in activist training at Highlander Folk School, an influential labor and civil rights training center in Tennessee. In contrast to the iconic imagery of Parks on the bus, these photographs have a homey, amateur feel to them. In the context of America in the 1950s, however, they are quite extraordinary. They show white and black activists working side-by-side and offer humble testimony to the hard, painstaking work of social change. In contrast to the image of the bus, which abstracts Parks from the community that called forth her heroism in the first place, the photos portray a diligent activist immersed in a larger movement. The success of the museum and library struck a raw nerve across town at Alabama State University, the state's oldest historically black university. TSU's campus is relatively new to Montgomery, and the university was staunchly lily white in the 1950s and 60s. In contrast, ASU faculty members—led by the likes of Joanne Robinson—were so deeply involved in the Movement that the university's budget was sacked by vindictive lawmakers, and the school temporarily lost its accreditation. From ASU's perspective, the Parks Library and Museum represents a cruelly ironic twist on the Movement's legacy.

12. Medgar Evers Memorial, Jackson, Mississippi.

Across the nation, the designers of civil rights memorials seek to influence collective memory by installing realistic statuary, informative plaques, and documentary photos. In contrast to much contemporary art—which can emphasize abstract expressionism and self-scrutiny at the expense of figural realism—most civil rights memorials are unabashedly referential; they seek to teach visitors about the past, not the process through which the past has come to be known. The Medgar Evers Memorial, on the grounds of the Medgar Evers branch library along Medgar Evers Boulevard, testifies to the efforts of designers to make the past manifest through literal repetition.

13. Medgar Evers's family residence, Jackson, Mississippi.

Often, memorial designers reinforce the sense of being in the presence of the past by linking collective memory with authentic places and personal artifacts. In the case of Medgar Evers, neither his namesake street nor his memorial (see Figure 12) has an immediate, lived connection to his activism and sacrifices. As a result, they lack the palatable gravitas of the driveway at his residence where he was assassinated by Byron De La Beckwirth in 1963. Geographer Kenneth Foote distinguishes between sites that have been "designated" and those that have been "sanctified." While the statue, library, and street have been designated, the site of his murder—if it should be sanctified in an appropriate fashion—has the potential to become a pilgrimage destination and, accordingly, to influence collective memory.

14. Statue of Martin Luther King, Jr., by Erik Blome, Milwaukee, Wisconsin.

In 1998, Milwaukee installed a statue of Dr. King created by Erik Blome, a nationally renowned sculptor. Placed alongside the street that bears King's name, Blome's work drew accolades from the community. In contrast, a second sculpture by Blome (see Figure 15) drew decidedly negative reactions from African Americans in Rocky Mount, North Carolina. The differing fate of each statue suggests the complexity of the politics surrounding the content of King's legacy and arguments over who should interpret it. (Photograph reprinted with the permission of Erik Blome.)

15. Statue of Martin Luther King, Jr., by Erik Blome, Rocky Mount, North Carolina.

In contrast to the vibrant physicality of Eric Blome's statue in Milwaukee (see Figure 14)—boldly striding forward, *Bible* in hand, calling the world to account—the statue in Rocky Mount depicted a contemplative King. For his part, Blome sought to imbue the statue in Rocky Mount with the gravity that characterized a 1962 photograph of King, one that reminded the artist of the somber, brooding mien of a king or judge. In response, African Americans in Rocky Mount issued a litany of complaints against the statue. Blome's depiction was criticized as depicting the civil rights leader as "arrogant" and, alternately, as "passive." Some thought the statue bore faint resemblance to the real man. In addition, Blome's racial identity became an issue when some community members questioned the ability of a white artist to represent properly King's legacy. Under pressure, officials in Rocky Mount cancelled the 2003 dedication ceremony and moved the statue to a city warehouse—a procedure that required a power hacksaw and the strenuous efforts of a municipal work crew. A second artist was hired, but his work launched a new round of vituperative criticism. The entire project was shelved until the city council, in May 2007, decided to reinstall Blome's statue. Reflecting on the affair, Blome argues that Rocky Mount officials did not do enough to bring the public into the design process. Further, he believes that there is no single, correct way to portray the civil rights leader. Inspired by King's habits of prayer, study, and contemplation—practices that girded his public persona—Blome sought to represent another side of King. As it happened, a vocal portion of Rocky Mount's African-American community disapproved of both the interpretation and the chosen interpreter. (Photograph reprinted with the permission of Erik Blome.)

16. Reliving the past at Clayborn Temple, Memphis, Tennessee.

This building's historical marker, erected by the Second Presbyterian Church and the Shelby County Commission in 1991, reads: "This building, designed by architects Long & Kees with E. C. Jones supervising, was dedicated to the worship of God on Jan. 1, 1893. It was the second home of Second Presbyterian Church (organized Dec. 28, 1844) until sold to the AME Church in 1949 and then renamed Clayborn Temple. Dr. Martin Luther King, Jr. often spoke here. Many civil rights activities were held here in the 1960's." Clayborn Temple was the spiritual and logistical center and the rallying point for the sanitation workers' strike that brought King to Memphis. On the evening of April 3, 1968, an exhausted Dr. King appeared at Clayborn Temple, where he delivered his last public address (known as the "I've been to the mountaintop" speech) that offers inspiration to us today. It was here where he declared, ". . . But I want you to know tonight, that we, as a people, will get to the Promised Land. And so I'm happy tonight; I'm not worried about anything; I'm not fearing any man. Mine eyes have seen the glory of the coming of the Lord. . . ." (as quoted in http://www.stanford. edu/group/King/publications/speeches/I've_been_to_the_mountaintop.pdf). The next day Dr. King was murdered in front of Room 306 on the balcony of the Lorraine Motel (see Figure 17), now the National Civil Rights Museum.

17. National Civil Rights Museum, Memphis, Tennessee.

A diverse coalition of state and private parties joined together to create a shrine and museum out of the Lorraine Motel where Dr. King was assassinated on April 4, 1968. Only a generation removed from its peak, the Civil Rights Movement is lauded in towns and cities whose names are synonymous with its triumph and tragedy. The speed with which civil rights sites have been officially commemorated masks the complex politics associated with their production. The trend toward celebrating America's multifarious heritage occurred neither spontaneously nor as a result of some inevitable force of history; rather, its origins are in the Movement and the concerted efforts of "memorial entrepreneurs": artists, authors, citizens, community organizers, corporate managers, elected officials, philanthropists, and scholars. Faced with the challenge of operating multi-million dollar facilities, civil rights museums must broaden their appeal beyond a national, pilgrimage-oriented audience by staging events that also attract a local audience with diverse interests. Thus note the marquee's reference to a temporary exhibit, "ALI: THE MAIN EVENT."

18. Clashing signs at the National Civil Rights Museum, Memphis, Tennessee.

Civil rights memorials simultaneously challenge and confirm the conventions that characterize commemoration in the United States. In this case, the pleading tone of the tourism economy ("!!We Are Open!!") runs headlong into the Civil Rights Movement's protest tradition ("STOP! Worshipping the Past, START! Living the Dream"). The latter sign is one of several deployed around the area by Jacqueline Smith (see Figure 19), a long-time poverty rights activist. She seeks to counter the museum's "business-as-usual" attitude toward commemoration, one that she believes promotes the passive consumption of history at the expense of revolutionary change. She would like to see the Lorraine Motel used as a local community resource rather than as a tourist draw for the city. More than 200,000 people visit the museum annually.

JACQUELINE SMITH
The last tenant of the Lorraine Hotel
HAS PROTESTED HERE FOR
14   123
Years   days

19. Jacqueline Smith outside the National Civil Rights Museum, Memphis, Tennessee.

Like those who complain that the mainstream portrait of the Movement marginalizes the contributions of women, grassroots activists, and workers, Smith's protest provides a point of contrast with the typical way of representing the past. For instance, she questions how the transformation of the Lorraine Motel (see Figure 17) from a low-budget motel that housed the poor into a tourist attraction actually supports Dr. King's beliefs in social and economic justice. The arrival of the Movement's memorial legacy on the cultural landscape serves as something of a litmus test for gauging how far society has come in actually "Living the Dream."

20. Broken King street sign, Woodland, Georgia.

This broken street sign in Woodland, Georgia, speaks to the degraded and poor conditions that are found on some streets honoring Dr. King. Woodland's memorial to King lies off of State Highway 41 along a small residential street that hosts a public housing project and, alarmingly nearby, a wastewater treatment facility. Many of the political dynamics that place noxious sites in poor, minority communities also lead to the marginalization of King's memory. Frequently, white opponents to street-renaming proposals state that they have no problem honoring Dr. King so long as it's "not on my street," an interesting corollary to the more famous NIMBYism ("not in my backyard") heard in many communities. An oft-cited fear is that property values will drop if one has a King address, although there is no evidence from appraisers to substantiate this claim. Rather than causing poverty, King's name often is placed in areas that are already struggling. The renaming of blighted and obscure streets has, in some instances, changed the streets' symbolic meaning from being a point of African-American pride to yet another reminder of continued racial inequality, what one journalist has called a "Boulevard of Broken Dreams." In the case of Woodland, a more fitting characterization may be a "Dream Turned Upside Down." (Photograph by Derek H. Alderman.)

21. Abandoned B. W. Cooper (Calliope) Housing Project, New Orleans, Louisiana.

The depressed condition of some King streets has led to the stereotypical view that all of them look like this. Such a stigma ignores the commercial prominence of some King streets while also giving white America permission to disregard the struggles and hardships that face people who live, work, and travel on King streets. Pictured here is the B. W. Cooper Housing Project on Martin Luther King Jr. Boulevard in New Orleans a month after Hurricane Katrina ravaged the Gulf Coast and displaced the thousands of poor African Americans who lived in the project. The apartments, even the few that were repaired, remain largely abandoned, and it has been difficult to entice residents to return. The situation has been complicated by the uncertainty of whether this and other housing projects will be redeveloped or demolished altogether. Well before Katrina, the Cooper apartments, formerly and more popularly known as the Calliope Projects, suffered from deterioration, gang wars, drug trafficking, and intense violence. The hurricane simply exposed and exacerbated longstanding patterns of inequality and hyper-segregation. From Calliope emerged rap mogul Master P and his brothers, Sikk the Shocker and C-Murder, who supposedly chose his stage name because of the murders he had witnessed. As journalist Jonathan Tilove has keenly observed: "To name any street for King is to invite an accounting of how the street makes good on King's promise or mocks it," (see note 37 on p. 116). The suffering associated with King Boulevard in New Orleans prompts us to consider how the Civil Rights Movement, both in terms of how it has changed society and how it is remembered, is a project that is far from being complete. (Photograph reprinted with the permission of Robert Walker.)

22. Memorial to slain students, South Carolina State University, Orangeburg.

While multimillion dollar facilities, such as those in Atlanta, Birmingham, and Memphis, attract the majority of visitors and public attention, this modest pedestal is perhaps more representative of the Civil Rights Movement's memorial landscape as a whole. Set near the entrance to SCSU's campus, the memorial quietly commemorates the "Orangeburg Massacre," a brief, violent chapter in the Movement's history. Its oblique language—the lives "taken" were those of three unarmed student protestors killed in a swarm of police bullets—and universalizing sentiments—the "pursuit of human dignity" as opposed to the calls for "Black Power" that rang out that night—suggests the raw, unfinished condition of the incident and the abiding conservatism of this small college town. Even the most humble memorials are places where competing versions of the past vie for attention in the present.

23. Martyr's stone, Voting Rights Park, Selma, Alabama.

This humble monument, set alongside a shaded path, recalls the names of nine lives lost in the struggle. The list embodies two features that characterize commemoration more broadly. First, its chiseled names evidence the widespread desire to produce collective memories capable of withstanding time's passage. Second, the list's contents attest that memorials, of necessity, can focus scarce attention on the particular at the expense of the whole, or vice versa. Since no memorial can be complete, visitors must figure out what is present and absent. In this case, the first four martyrs—Jackson, Liuzzo (see Figure 75), Reeb, and Daniels (in order of presentation on the stone)—were killed in the events leading up to, and immediately following, the 1965 Voting Rights March. As if the testimony of their lives was not enough, the stone goes on to record the names of five individuals slain not in Alabama, but over the course of several years in Mississippi: Evers (see Figures 12 and 13), Schwerner, Chaney, Goodman, and Young. Remarkably, Dr. King's name is absent from the list, a rare omission that likely reflects the park's emphasis on voting rights and its founders' ambivalence regarding King's dominance over the Movement's legacy.

24. Edmund Pettus Bridge, Selma, Alabama.

Technically, this span across the Alabama River preserves the memory of Mr. Pettus, a Confederate general and racist U.S. Senator. In popular memory, however, it is known as the site of "Bloody Sunday," the police riot on March 25, 1965, that tilted public opinion nationwide in favor of voting rights activists. This dramatic shift in what might be thought of as the bridge's commemorative "moorings" is an example of the manner in which a memorial can betray its founders' intentions. By virtue of their gravitas—both literal and figurative—memorials seemingly promise to place the past beyond the vagaries of time. Yet, a memorial cannot speak for itself; it relies on an audience's interpretation, and its signification can change accordingly. Thus, even a straightforward memorial—a bridge named after a patrician white supremacist—is capable of betraying its origins. Moreover, the potential for reversal endures: "The Malcolm X Grassroots Movement" chose Selma's annual Bridge Crossing Jubilee across the Pettus Bridge as the backdrop for protesting a speech by the Reverend Jesse Jackson. The group complained that Jackson's message and tactics—symbolized by the bridge's allusions to nonviolent protest—were hopelessly outmoded. The contrast between their stark visibility and tremulous meaning makes memorials inviting targets for activists seeking to broadcast their message.

25. Civil rights mural, Selma, Alabama.

This mural on concrete blocks is an example of the kind of public place that is dedicated to the life and work of Dr. King. The Edmund Pettus Bridge (see Figure 24) appears above King's head, like a halo. The mural was created by students enrolled in a youth-oriented program called "Freedom Summer," offering testimony to the importance that activists place on memorial entrepreneurialism, not to overlook the talents of the students and their mentors.

IN MEMORY OF:
REVEREND HOSEA WILLIAMS, SR.
LEADER OF
THE SELMA-MONTGOMERY MARCH
MARCH 25, 1965

"UNBOSSED AND UNBOUGHT"
1926–2000
Presented by:
SCLC/W.O.M.E.N., INC.
Women's Organizational Movement for Equality Now
EVELYN G. LOWERY, FOUNDER/CHAIR
March 3, 2002

26. Hosea Williams, Sr., Memorial to Voting Rights Park, Selma, Alabama.

The past is a fungible commodity, suitably flexible to fit present circumstances, in this case the desire of the Southern Christian Leadership Conference (SCLC) to shape the Movement's memorial legacy. As a field organizer for the SCLC, Hosea Williams, Sr. assisted local activists organizing what became the Voting Rights March. Activists set out from Selma for Montgomery on three separate occasions, only reaching their destination on the third attempt, with Dr. King, not Williams, at the head of column. Williams and John Lewis, of the Student Non-Violent Coordinating Committee, led the first march, getting no further than the Edmund Pettus Bridge (see Figure 24), where they were set upon by baton-wielding state troopers. News cameras recorded the ambush, and the subsequent images were deemed sensational enough that ABC interrupted its broadcast of *Judgment at Nuremberg*, a film about Nazi Germany, to report on violent antics uncomfortably closer to home.

27. Sixteenth Street Baptist Church, Birmingham, Alabama.

In the wake of successful protests in Birmingham, the then-shaky coalition planning the March on Washington gathered strength and, in turn, spurred on passage of the landmark Civil Rights Act of 1964, spearheaded by President Lyndon Baynes Johnson. In response, the Ku Klux Klan, on September 15, 1963, dynamited Sixteenth Street Baptist Church, killing four girls who were making ready for worship: Addie Mae Collins (age fourteen), Denise McNair (age eleven), Carole Robertson (age fourteen), and Cynthia Wesley (age fourteen).

28. Memorial plaque and flowers, Sixteenth Street Baptist Church, Birmingham, Alabama.

The Sixteenth Street Baptist Church (see Figure 27)—designated a "National Treasure" by the federal government and undergoing extensive renovations as a result—has assumed a central place in the Movement's collective memory. Among the many memorials dedicated to commemorating its role, the two interior pictures shown here and in Figure 29 give a sense of the spatial extent of its impact. The first (above) is a bronze plaque accompanied by plastic flowers that sits on a table in the church's basement bookshop, a humble reminder of the many years the church quietly commemorated the girls' tragic deaths. The second (Figure 29) is an ornate stained-glass window in the church's balcony—"A gift from the people of Wales"—that speaks to the international dimensions of the incident's commemoration. The simple dignity of both memorials is a poignant reminder of how the Movement was remembered before the growth of heritage tourism and its multimedia flash.

YOU DO IT TO ME

GIVEN BY THE PEOPLE OF WALES U.K MCMLXIV

29. Memorial window, Sixteenth Street Baptist Church, Birmingham, Alabama.

30. Kelly Ingram Park, Birmingham, Alabama.

Assigning history a place on the cultural landscape gives it a tangible presence. Kelly Ingram Park has been reworked in order to shape collective memory. At one time segregated for the use of whites only, the park is closely associated with the Civil Rights Movement. It was the site at which Bull Conner's police attacked protesters—many of them children—with fierce dogs and powerful fire hoses in 1963. Redesigned and dedicated as a "PLACE OF REVOLUTION AND RECONCILIATION" in 1992 by Richard Arrington, the city's first African-American mayor, the park commemorates the protests that desegregated the city. The project's designers sought to remind future generations that no meaningful reconciliation in Birmingham could be achieved between the races without a revolution in their relationship—no justice, no peace. Likewise, the gains of the revolution would be pyrrhic if the result was an embittered division, a point not lost on perceptive observers of a Birmingham whose schools, residences, and churches are nearly as segregated today as they were a half century ago, albeit this time without the law's backing.

31. Statuary, Kelly Ingram Park, Birmingham, Alabama.

32. Statuary, Kelly Ingram Park, Birmingham, Alabama.

Geographer Kenneth Foote, whose research on places of violence and tragedy is well known, describes the ways that landscapes can be reworked either to clarify or to obscure the events associated with them. For instance, Kelly Ingram Park offers a public primer in the Movement's fundamental tactic: the orchestrated confrontation between the innocence of nonviolent protest and the brutal response of unveiled white supremacy. Paved with slabs of flinty black slate, a narrow walkway circumscribes the park. It is not possible to enter the park's contemplative center without confronting the menacingly large sculptures that straddle the path. The close, visceral presence of the statuary along the walkway—which are not abstract shapes but frighteningly realistic dogs (see Figure 31) and water cannons (see Figure 35)—offers a poignant study in opposites. The hulking jail and lunging dogs are opposed by nothing more than the budding courage of children, shown above. That a commemorative statuary park occupies the ground of a pivotal moment in the Civil Rights Movement is a telling sign of how the struggle was resolved.

33. King Memorial, Kelly Ingram Park, Birmingham, Alabama.

Architectural historian Dell Upton has observed that Kelly Ingram Park's diagonal paths reflect contrasting approaches to the pursuit of social justice. Along one path, a statue of Martin Luther King, Jr. bears solemn witness to the confrontational nature of nonviolent protest, silently beckoning to Sixteenth Street Baptist Church's elite congregation to embrace the tactics of direct action. The park's other axis speaks to a different strategy for making good on democracy's promise.

34. Carrie A. Tuggle Memorial, Kelly Ingram Park, Birmingham, Alabama.

Anchored by four, charcoal-gray stelae, this corner of the park faces Fourth Avenue, historically the center of Birmingham's African–American business community. Inscribed with a name, brief testimony, and bronze, low-relief profile, each stela recounts the efforts of a black professional to serve Birmingham's African-American community. In the case of philanthropist and educator Carrie A. Tuggle, a stela commemorates her advocacy on behalf of orphans and juvenile defendants. The subdued character of the stelae embodies a conservative approach to progress—one that eschewed confrontation and looked to accommodate multiple interests through quiet negotiations and the accumulation of wealth. What, on the surface, appears to be a single testimony to the Movement is, in fact, a complex meditation on divergent political traditions within black Birmingham, writ large on and through the park.

35. Statuary, Kelly Ingram Park, Birmingham, Alabama.

This statuary of a water canon reminds visitors of the brutal action taken by Bull Conner's police force in 1963, when civil rights protesters—both adults and children—were viciously assaulted in this park by Birmingham's finest.

36. Mural of the Old South, Jefferson County Courthouse, Birmingham, Alabama.

Traditionally, American public history reflected the hopes and plans of white elites. These murals, produced by John Norton in 1931, are a case in point. When they were not ignored altogether, African Americans were included as bit characters whose presence testified to the centrality of whites. In the "Mural of the Old South" (above), black field hands and liveried servants support the matronly embodiment of the Old South. In the "Mural of the New South" (see Figure 37), the black presence is simultaneously diminished and sent underground, as the white working class provides the foundation for the New South's confident gaze toward the future.

37. Mural of the New South, Jefferson County Courthouse, Birmingham, Alabama.

In the wake of the Civil Rights Movement and the arrival of black elected officials, calls to remove these murals of the Old and New Souths have been made. Outright removal, however, would destroy a "material witness" to white supremacy's pervasiveness, depriving future generations of a piece of their collective past. Perhaps a counter-mural or plaque—something like Liberty Monument in New Orleans—might be an appropriate way to reverse an otherwise repugnant element of the past.

38. African-American monument, Savannah, Georgia.

Challenges to the Won Cause rendition of the Civil Rights Movement have led not only to a greater recognition of the ordinary and previously nameless figures in the Movement, but also to a desire to place the struggle for civil rights within a broader and more critical historical context. For instance, in Savannah, Abigail Jordan, an African-American activist, led a decade-long campaign to build a monument commemorating what she called the "invisible story" of the trans-Atlantic slave trade. The city already had a civil rights museum and a street named for Dr. King, but Jordan deemed that these memorials celebrated specific leaders and failed to capture the struggles and achievements of the black community as a whole. More importantly, she argued that Savannah's slave memorial, unlike these other African-American monuments, would not isolate the struggle for racial equality as a moment in time but would portray it as part of a larger, African-American journey "that began as a forced voyage across the sea and transformed into an undeniable call for freedom." It is an unfinished journey, according to Jordan, and she implores fellow African Americans to recognize the still evolving nature of the Movement. On this point, she has said: "Don't just lean back and say, 'Oh, we have made it.' Black folk have not arrived as of yet."

39. Memorial to John Hunt Morgan, Lexington, Kentucky.

To the extent they were able, African Americans nurtured an alternative to the dominant white history. For African Americans, remembering both injustice and better times was vital to maintaining a sense of identity and purpose. As anti-apartheid activists in the context of South Africa observed, "Ours is the struggle of remembering against forgetting." For instance, the courthouse lawn in Lexington, Kentucky, celebrates the exploits of Confederate cavalry officer John Hunt Morgan. In contrast, African Americans have long memorialized the site among themselves as the location of the nation's largest trans-Appalachian slave market. Their countermemorial is a reminder that the act of commemoration is inherently *partial*. Memorials are *incomplete*, in that they can only make partial selections from the whole cloth of the past; they are *biased*, inasmuch as this imperative to cut and abstract leads inevitably to partiality toward one version of the past or the other. Thus, memorials bear *partial* witness to the past, calling attention to some portion of the narratives associated with a place and, in the process, often obscuring other, sometimes competing memories.

THERE IS GLORY

GLOOM

1807 ROBERT E. LEE 1870

ROBERT N. PHILPOT   PHILLIP RAIFORD   ISAAC B. HOWARD
SELMA HOME GUARD OXFORD GRAYS, MISS.   20 MISS. INFANTRY
APRIL 2. 1865   BORN 1837   DIED 1924 BORN 1842 DIED 1920

40. Confederate Soldiers Memorial, Selma, Alabama.

Glenn Eskew, a historian of the American South, characterizes the predominant framing of the Movement as the "Won Cause." Told in contrast to the Lost Cause of the Confederacy—of which the inscription on Selma's monument to its Confederate dead, "There is grandeur in graves, there is glory in gloom," is a fulsome example—the Won Cause represents the Movement as a story of sweeping cultural and political triumphs.

41. African-American Memorial on the capitol grounds, Columbia, South Carolina.

By historical retelling, heroic figures—such as the satisfied foursome portrayed on the capitol grounds in Columbia—overcame racist violence and official malfeasance to enjoy full membership in America's middle class. This interpretive framework predominates at civil rights memorials despite abundant evidence that nothing about the Movement was preordained.

The Civil Rights Movement was Launched Based on Rights Afforded by the Emancipation Proclamation and the Constitution.

17 May 1954 Supreme Court outlaws school segregation in Brown vs. Board of Education.

1 Dec 1955 Rosa Parks arrested for refusing to give up her seat on bus to a white man.

5 Dec 1955 Montgomery bus boycott begins.

13 Nov 1956 Supreme Court bans segregated seating on Montgomery buses.

29 Aug 1957 Congress passes first Civil Rights Act since reconstruction.

24 Sep 1957 President Eisenhower orders federal troops to enforce school desegregation.

1 Feb 1960 Black students stage sit-in at "Whites Only" lunch counter.

5 Dec 1960 Supreme Court outlaws segregation in bus terminal.

1 Apr 1962 Civil Rights groups join forces to launch voter registration drive.

3 May 1963 Birmingham police attack marching children with dogs and hoses.

11 Jun 1963 Alabama Governor stands in schoolhouse door to stop university integration.

28 Aug 1963 250,000 Americans march on Washington for Civil Rights.

23 Jan 1964 Poll tax outlawed in Federal elections.

20 Jun 1964 Freedom summer brings 1,000 young Civil Rights volunteers to Mississippi.

2 Jul 1964 President Johnson signs Civil Rights Act of 1964.

21 Feb 1965 Malcolm X was assassinated in the presence of his family in N.Y.

7 Mar 1965 State Troopers beat back marchers at Edmund Pettus Bridge.

25 Mar 1965 Civil Rights march from Selma to Montgomery completed.

9 Jul 1965 Congress passes voting Rights Act of 1965.

2 Oct 1967 Thurgood Marshall sworn in as first Black Supreme Court Justice.

4 Apr 1968 Dr. Martin Luther King, Jr., preparing to lead a demonstration, was assassinated in Memphis.

NATIONAL EVENTS

42. Civil Rights Memorial, Albany, Georgia.

This monument in Albany—with its typographic echoes of Maya Lin's work in Montgomery—embodies the Won Cause's sense of inevitability as the Movement transforms the South at seemingly preordained times and places: Birmingham, Greensboro, Little Rock, Memphis, Montgomery, Selma, and Topeka. Importantly, the narrative's *leitmotif* alternates between moods of elation (such as the Voting Rights March of 1965) and tragedy (such as the assassination of Martin Luther King, Jr.). Desegregation was achieved in Albany after protests, whites reneging on earlier agreements, and a famous defeat: Martin Luther King, Jr. suffered a rare setback here, partly a result of divisions among the NAACP, the SNCC, and King's SCLC.

43. Shiloh Baptist Church, Albany, Georgia.

Many sites lay claim to the distinction of being the Movement's origin. For instance, Montgomery, Alabama, Topeka, Kansas, and Greensboro, North Carolina (see Figure 60), are among these many sites. Shiloh Baptist Church makes a parallel, if somewhat less expansive, claim on public memory: "THE ALBANY CIVIL RIGHTS MOVEMENT STARTED HERE"—a claim substantiated by the fact that the church hosted the campaign's first mass meeting in 1961. Yet, is it really possible to identify the geographic origin of something as complex as a political movement? In the case of Albany, why not instead identify the private home where activists first gathered or the site of the first acts of civil disobedience as the origin? The answer lies in part with the fact that Albany's civil rights museum sits across the street in what was a rival church.

44. Memorial to slaves loyal to the Confederacy, Fort Hill, South Carolina.

Like a book, memorial landscapes can be "read." Unlike conventional books, however, the "pages" of a memorial landscape reflect the efforts of multiple "authors" to convey a message to the future. Jim Carrier, in *A Traveler's Guide to the Civil Rights Movement*, calls attention to a patch of civic greenspace near the center of Fort Hill that recreates the memorial landscape of so many Southern towns, with a twist. Amid the cannons and battle flags, a modest limestone obelisk honors those "faithful slaves" who upheld their "sacred trust" during the "struggle for the principles of our Confederate States of America." The obelisk was erected in 1895 as whites in the region simultaneously proclaimed the first incarnation of the New South and toasted the reign of Jim Crow. The images and text are in keeping with the longstanding practice of marginalizing African Americans through minstrelsy and tales of happy slaves. The memorial, however, sits uneasily against a backdrop of tony shops that have taken up residence along the Main Street of this hamlet-cum-bedroom-suburb of Charlotte, North Carolina.

45. "NO ROOM FOR RACISM" street sign, Rock Hill, South Carolina.

Like Atlanta, Georgia which proclaimed itself "Too Busy to Hate" during the violence that accompanied desegregation elsewhere in the region, the rapidly expanding metropolitan area of Charlotte, North Carolina, fancies itself an avatar of the latest incarnation of the New South, one that is post-racism and pro-diversity. In keeping with this sentiment, nearby Rock Hill informs visitors that it is "A CITY THAT HAS NO ROOM FOR RACISM." Geographers study the memorial landscape in its spatial context in order to appreciate the "in-between" condition of places such as Charlotte that cannot help but be partially Old South and partially New South.

46. Emancipation Memorial, Washington Park, Washington, D.C.

When not ignored altogether, African Americans were commonly portrayed on the cultural landscape as passive rather than active agents. Art historian Kirk Savage's research on the Civil War's memorial legacy reported that the handful of monuments from this period that portray African Americans represent them in the diminutive vis-à-vis whites. Cast as such, the inclusion of blacks on the cultural landscape ironically served to reinforce, rather than undermine, racial ideology. Such is the case in this memorial, and in the monument at Tuskegee (see Figure 47), where crouching black figures attest to the self-conceit by which whites appointed themselves history's agent. In Washington Park, Abraham Lincoln's beneficent countenance and the freedman's bent knee obscure not only the leading role slaves played in slavery's demise, but also Lincoln's cool indifference to their plight.

47. Booker T. Washington monument, Tuskegee, Alabama.

The contrast between the propriety of Booker T. Washington's dress and carriage and the crouching nakedness of the race confirms his agency. While Washington is, of course, literally a black man, in the eyes of his white patrons his was the ideal black life: lifted up from indolent slavery into the industrious ways of white folk. Thus, in this monument and the one in Washington Park (see Figure 46), the composition's agency resides with the standing "white" figure while the black race is rendered passively reliant. Presciently, radicals, such as Frederick Douglass and W. E. B. DuBois, criticized both statues' silence regarding the forces arrayed against African Americans, such as slaveholders, agrarian peonage, and post-Reconstruction racism.

48. "Freedom Road," King National Historic Site, Atlanta, Georgia.

There is a longstanding practice of using allegorical figures to confirm an individual's character and destiny: in the absence of the passive supplicant, neither the greatness of Abraham Lincoln (see Figure 46) nor Booker T. Washington (see Figure 47) could be known. Something similar plays out on the civil rights memorial landscape. The vast majority of the Movement's participants—both men and women—stand in powerful but silent testimony to the heroic qualities of Movement leaders, such as Dr. King. For instance, the mannequin marchers depicted in "Freedom Road" confirm King's leadership as they forever stride toward his crypt (see Figure 52), which lies a short distance beyond the window. The positions of allegorical figures—whether kneeling in supplication, crouching in ignorance, or loyally following—serve to confirm a leader's greatness. In contrast to the figures pictured above, note the different mood struck by the allegorical figure of Kunta Kinte from *Roots* in "Behold" (see Figure 49), who is depicted not only acknowledging his paternity, but also asking the Creator to bless his daughter, Kizzy.

49. "Behold," King National Historic Site, Atlanta, Georgia.

"Behold" was an unsolicited gift to the King National Historic Site, but King family members and the historic site's superintendent questioned the statue's artistic merit and relevance. In contrast to the lifecast marchers in "Freedom Road" (see Figure 48), however, "Behold" is a popular site for photos, as many children, and probably not a few adults, mistakenly assume that the statue depicts Dr. King! For their part, the lifecast marchers are routinely vandalized, and their taupe coloring draws a rare note of criticism from visitors (such as, "Why aren't they blacker?").

50. King's birth home, King National Historic Site, Atlanta, Georgia.

In addition to the national holiday and hundreds of public places dedicated to his memory (see Figure 25), most of the places associated with Dr. King's life and career have become memorials in much the same fashion as have places linked to other great men and women, such as George Washington, Abraham Lincoln, Jane Addams, and Harriet Beecher Stowe. Among these sites are his birthplace in Atlanta and the family's residence in Montgomery (see Figure 51). Tours of King's birth home are given hourly most days of the year; the tour emphasizes the King family's middle-class lifestyle.

51. King family residence, Montgomery, Alabama.

Civil rights memorials are not alone in telling history from the perspective of leaders and elite organizations. The commemoration of Martin Luther King, Jr. on the cultural landscape reflects the pervasive influence of what is teasingly referred to as the "Great Man" style of retelling history. This framework aggrandizes leaders, heroes, and national organizations rather than grassroots organizers and local participants. As the shadows stretching across the lawn of the family's residence in Montgomery attest, heritage tourists seek out sites associated with King's life. In a manner reminiscent of the Jefferson Davis marker on the Alabama capitol's porch (see Figure 8), a bronze plaque on the manse's porch notes the spot where a would-be assassin's bomb landed.

52. Martin Luther King, Jr.'s crypt, King Center for Nonviolent Change, Atlanta, Georgia.

Hundreds of thousands visit Dr. King's crypt annually, but few choose to linger in a place that is so hostile to contemplation. With its moat and gleaming stone, it is a hard, cold place for a man of the people. Who will take charge of this site as his peers pass on? In 2006, the crypt was enlarged to include Dr. King's wife, Coretta Scott King (1927–2006).

53. Site of the planned King Memorial near the Mall in Washington, D.C.

Public sites related to the Movement have become so numerous that it is perhaps easy to take their future for granted. As David Vann, former Birmingham mayor and Civil Rights Institute supporter commented, "I've always said the best way to put bad images to rest is to declare them history and put them in a museum" (see note 9 on p. 119). What effect has this sentiment had on sites related to Martin Luther King, Jr.? Like any artistic work, a memorial represents a point of view chosen from among many, often competing, perspectives. In truth, it is simply impossible to represent everything at once; selection is necessary. The emphatic manner in which most civil rights memorials make these choices—the genre is not known for its subtlety—offers insight into what their producers value and disparage. That said, what shape will the proposed memorial to Dr. King near the Mall in Washington, D.C., take? What themes will it reveal? Which themes will it ignore and conceal?

54. King memorial on the grounds of Brown Chapel, Selma, Alabama.

In this scene from Selma, we see the monument that renders Dr. King's signature line in the past tense, "I HAD A DREAM." There is a gap in age between the docent and her audience. Will this scene be repeated in a generation?

55. Graffiti, Auburn Avenue, Atlanta, Georgia.

That memorials come in all shapes and sizes is an obvious fact. In the context of American public space, however, the site and situation of a memorial is a reliable indicator of both the influence of those who installed it and the normative power of its message. A memorial erected in public space must exceed a higher threshold of approval, governmental and otherwise, than other forms of commemoration. As such, a public memorial is a very demanding kind of media, inasmuch as it cannot simply be purchased and "installed," as is the case with a bumper sticker, emblazoned T-shirt, or graffiti tag. Thus, the dramatic contrast between the hastily scrawled "memorial" across an abandoned building on behalf of Jamil Al-Amin (né H. Rap Brown) in the wake of his arrest and the King National Historic Site (see Figures 48–50), which lies a short distance further along Auburn Avenue, acts as something of a yardstick for measuring the relative popularity of their respective messages and constituencies. The comparison intuitively suggests the presence of vastly differing quantities of influence over territory on the part of the "gangs"-cum-memorial-entrepreneurs who erected them. That said, two caveats regarding size and the memorial landscape are worth noting. First, while messages that do not fit into the mold of the Won Cause and Great Man versions of the Movement are commonly denied access to public space, they do find ways onto the cultural landscape via less authoritative media, such as bumper stickers. As it happens, bumper stickers are a way of turning private property into a memorial of sorts but with a much lower threshold of access to the public sphere. Second, no memorial, however "small," deserves to be ignored. As a sign of care, all memorials matter to the people who created and visit them. Whereas size and political capital are proportional, size and care are not. As such, all memorials—ranging from t-shirts celebrating Nat Turner's rebellion to multimillion dollar museums—reveal something of the people associated with them. Thus, murals and graffiti are potentially as informative as a full-scale museum, albeit more transitory.

56. Moving Star Hall, Johns Island, South Carolina.

The controversy over how best to remember the Movement extends to debates over the types of places worthy of preservation. While the sweeping grandeur of the March on Washington, D.C., epitomizes the Movement for many—the very spot from which King delivered his "I have a dream" speech is now marked (see Figure 1)—others want to preserve more mundane places where activists found sustenance, developed tactics, and built community. Places deserving preservation by dint of their service to the Movement include Moving Star Hall, one of Septima Clark's original Freedom Schools—the unglamorous, grassroots base for the Movement's voting rights campaign. At present, the building serves as a chapel; nearby development by well-to-do retirees endangers its future.

57. All-Star Bowling, Orangeburg, South Carolina.

Robert Weyeneth, a professor of historic preservation at the University of South Carolina and a pioneering scholar in the study of the Movement's commemoration, has observed that no systematic efforts are currently being made by state and local preservation agencies to document and inventory the numerous places associated with the Movement, many of which are not otherwise noteworthy. Journalist Jim Carrier has observed that seemingly mundane places are crucial, because the stories associated with them allow for a richer understanding of the Movement's inner workings; they also provide a venue to celebrate the uncommon valor of ordinary participants in the Movement, thereby making visible the role of women and working-class activists who are otherwise overlooked. Essentially, when the places that nurtured and sustained activism are not commemorated, the Movement's legacy is narrowed to a handful of marquee events. A happy exception is the All-Star bowling lanes in Orangeburg, near the campus of South Carolina State University. The segregation of this bowling alley was the proximate cause of student demonstrations that ended in the shooting deaths of three protestors by police (see Figure 22). Today, the lanes are listed on the National Register of Historic Places, an example of the canon of places considered to be properly "historical," expanding in the Movement's wake.

58. Martin Luther King, Jr. Water Monument, King Memorial Garden, Raleigh, North Carolina.

Civil rights memorials typically do not call attention to ambiguous motives, painful doubts, or alternative interpretation; rather, they bear witness to what happened, to whom, and where. As such, most civil rights memorials act as memory aids: they seek to make tangible the past itself, not to promote insights into how our knowledge of the past comes to be. Maya Lin's striking installation in Montgomery (see page ii) displays an ambivalence that is generally lacking on the memorial landscape. Her design for that memorial—the names of individuals who died in the Movement bathed in water and etched into a table of black marble—echoes her approach to the Vietnam War Memorial in Washington, D.C. In this sense, both memorials are exceptionally literal; but whereas the Vietnam Memorial's linearity suggests a beginning and an end, the ellipsoid, sundial appearance of her Civil Rights Memorial in Montgomery combines with the unceasing cascade to suggest a cycle of death and rebirth, endlessly witnessed by the healing, mourning waters. More typical of the genre's stolid mien is this memorial garden in Raleigh designed by Bruce Lightner, son of Clarence Lightner who is memorialized on the monument. While he borrows liberally from Lin's inspired design, the outcome is more uneven. The memorial strikes a celebratory tone, literally cramming the twelve-ton granite table—predictably bathed in water—with the names of twenty-five local notables who made significant achievements with regard to civil rights, race relations, community improvements, and the quality of public education.

59. King Memorial Garden, Raleigh, North Carolina.

The emphasis on individual recognition extends into the present via a brick wall on which donations to the memorial garden are recognized with etched bricks, some of which have been enhanced—in the case of the Yarborough Family with an ink pen—to call attention to their contribution. A bronze plaque at the site inexplicably identifies 1966 as the Movement's culmination. Whereas a palpable tension between loss and gain sparks Lin's monument, most civil rights memorials emphasize success and a staid reporting of events and people. The sad result is a surfeit of eminently forgettable monuments. In the absence of either controversy or novelty, these sites risk irrelevancy. If the Movement itself marked a radical break with the past, to what extent should its memorials do the same?

BIRTHPLACE OF THE CIVIL RIGHTS MOVEMENT
Four students at North Carolina A & T State
University conducted the first lunch counter sit-in
on February 1, 1960 at the Woolworth Store.

Franklin McCain   Joseph McNeil
Ezell Blair, Jr.   David Richmond
"Sometimes taking a stand for what is
undeniably right means taking a seat."
Presented to the City of Greensboro by Radio Stations
WEAL and WQMG February 1, 1990

Huff Art Studio

60. Historic marker, Greensboro, North Carolina.

Greensboro is one of the sites that lay claim to being the Civil Rights Movement's origin. Other cities include Topeka, Kansas, Montgomery, Alabama, and Albany, Georgia (see Figure 43).

61. Woolworth's door, Greensboro, North Carolina.

Two of the most common questions posed by visitors to civil rights memorials reflect their desire to forge an authentic, visceral connection with the past being depicted: "Is this real? Is this what it was really like?" As a result, memorial entrepreneurs seek out opportunities to emphasize their site's bona fides. A case in point is the International Civil Rights Center and Museum in Greensboro, North Carolina, which is under development. While the actual stools and counter from the sit-in at Woolworth's Department Store reside at the Smithsonian Institution in Washington, D.C., the museum will rely on the few remaining original items, such as the Woolworth's door and floor tiles, to give visitors the sense that they are touching history.

62. Window display, International Civil Rights Center and Museum, Greensboro, North Carolina.

Housed in the same building that Woolworth's occupied at the time of the lunch counter sit-in protests, the International Civil Rights Center and Museum reinforces Greensboro's claim to have launched a national and, eventually, worldwide struggle for human rights. This window display at the museum encapsulates the typical trajectory of the Movement as having grown out of a longstanding tradition of activism (represented by the early-twentieth-century anti-lynching banner) to become a mass movement (King leading the 1963 March on Washington) that would eventually inspire similar campaigns around the world, including the now iconic image of a pro-democracy protestor, on June 5, 1989, squaring off against a Peoples' Liberation Army tank in Tiananmen Square in Beijing. Like many other memorials, the museum in Greensboro presents the international arena as the Movement's next frontier. Doing so, however, has the unfortunate effect of distracting attention from ongoing civil rights struggles closer to home: contemporary racism, voting rights/fraud, and criminal (in)justice.

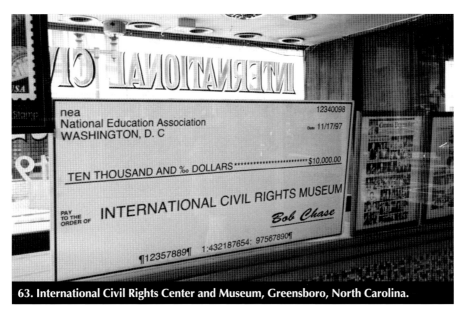

63. International Civil Rights Center and Museum, Greensboro, North Carolina.

The International Civil Rights Center and Museum was initiated by the energetic efforts of McArthur Davis, who offers a different take on the role of the memorial entrepreneur. Typically, memorials are created by multiple parties who often agree on little more than it being right to erect a memorial; the memorial's location, form, and content, however, remain matters of great debate. The odd bedfellows of local government, businesses, labor unions, philanthropists, and civil rights activists that have come together in Greensboro to commemorate the Movement offers testimony to Davis's motivation and diplomatic acumen.

64. Street corner, Greensboro, North Carolina.

In 1979, a Ku Klux Klan assault on a civil rights and labor march in Greensboro resulted in the deaths of three activists, but the site remains unmarked. The quiet street corner at Carver and Jennifer where the killings took place—and the extent to which the shocking incident continues to divide whites and blacks in Greensboro—stands in dramatic contrast to the multi-million dollar International Civil Rights Center and Museum (see Figures 61–63) taking shape in town. The different treatment of these sites—one embraced, the other shunned—reflects in microcosm the uneven treatment that the Movement receives on the cultural landscape when the local "present" is too controversial for museums to handle.

65. Dynamic Metals lofts, corner of Edgemont and Randolph streets, Atlanta, Georgia.

Certain neighborhoods may look similarly decrepit, but their trajectories are radically different. Whereas the neighborhood along Jackson's Civil Rights Tour (see Figures 66 and 67) shows all the signs of economic disinvestment and social distress, the proposed upscale lofts on the site formerly occupied by Dynamic Metals in Atlanta testifies to the way gentrification can radically alter neighborhoods near historic civil rights sites. Could you afford to live here?

66. Civil Rights Tour, Site 32, Jackson, Mississippi.

Making sense out of a memorial begins with careful observation of the artifact's environs. What kind of neighborhood did you travel through to get here? What surrounds the memorial: interstates and warehouses? Abandoned apartment blocks? A bustling business district? Gentrified lofts and condos? Would you feel comfortable walking around the neighborhood? Would you want to live here?

The Infamous
Country Boy Clique POWDER
The Album
IN STORES NOW!

67. Heritage tourists along the Civil Rights Tour, Jackson, Mississippi.

68. Greyhound Bus station, Montgomery, Alabama.

In his survey of landscapes marred by tragedy, geographer Kenneth Foote observed that a site's treatment can vary in relation to trends in heritage tourism and the politics of memory. The two sites pictured here— the bus station (above) in Montgomery where Freedom Riders were mauled and the grocery store in Money (see Figure 69) where Emmett Till's murderers alleged he sassed a white woman—exemplify the fluid manner in which a site can shift position among Foote's categories of sanctification, designation, rehabilitation, and obliteration. The bus station was initially rehabilitated, inasmuch as it continued to function as a depot. Later, it became a government office building and was marked with a historic plaque. It seems, however, to be destined for sanctification, as the state plans to acquire the building, restore it, and establish it as a shrine and interpretive center dedicated to the Freedom Riders.

69. Abandoned grocery store, Money, Mississippi.

Although this building in Money continued to function as a grocery in the wake of Emmett Till's murder and the exoneration of his killers, presently it has been abandoned and is quickly sliding into obliteration. The fact that heritage tourists seek it out, however, suggests its potential for sanctification, especially given the growing importance of Till's murder as the search for the Movement's origins moves beyond Topeka, Montgomery, Greensboro, and Albany. The apparently senseless violence associated with both sites—a young man murdered for flirting and bus riders beaten for choosing the wrong seats—lends itself to the Won Cause's retelling of the Movement as the triumph of reason and right over senseless violence and hatred. The fact that these sites of atrocity and suffering haven't received the same treatment as more victorious places—and probably won't—reflects each site's local context. Whereas Alabama's presentation of civil rights history as "heritage" is part of the state's economic development strategy, Mississippi has been unwilling to capitalize on its sites associated with the Won Cause, perhaps because the Cause hasn't yet been won in the Magnolia State.

70. Ohio Historical Marker, Miami University, Oxford, Ohio.

The dictum attributed to Tip O'Neil, former Speaker of the House of Representatives, that "all politics are local" is as true with regard to the Won Cause retelling of the Civil Rights Movement as it is in the halls of Congress. A case in point is the handsome amphitheater and official plaque on Miami University's campus that commemorate events associated with the 1964 Freedom Summer campaign. Before departing for Mississippi, Freedom Summer volunteers received activist training in Oxford. The plaque notes that three of those activists were subsequently murdered near Philadelphia (Greek for "brotherly love"), Mississippi. Nothing more formal than a small, privately financed plaque marks the event in Philadelphia; anything more substantial has thus far proved impossible to install. The disparate treatment of the event derives in part from the Won Cause's framing of the Movement as a story of good versus evil in which the good guys stand for progress, reason, and justice, while the bad guys are wedded to ignorance, fear, and bigotry. While this framework is gripping, the contrast between Oxford and Philadelphia suggests that it does not lend itself to retelling in every locale, especially those where civil rights remain unfinished business. In Philadelphia, the Won Cause's need for "bad guys" raises uncomfortable questions about the past for many Mississippians—black and white. No such burden exists in Oxford, where the accusatory finger points comfortably southward. That said, Philadelphia isn't the only place with unresolved civil rights issues. In the same year that dead bodies were turning up across the South, a bulldozer crushed and killed Bruce Klunder, a civil rights activist protesting a segregated school in Cleveland, Ohio. Telling of the Won Cause's limitations, the only memorial to Klunder's strange, untimely death is hundreds of miles away in Montgomery, Alabama, where Maya Lin included his name among those of forty-eight martyrs to the cause (see page ii). The Won Cause offers memorial entrepreneurs a way to distinguish themselves from the past and to project a progressive image into the future if, and only if, there is a local consensus that the event is comfortably distant in either time or space. The Won Cause doesn't lend itself to a local discussion of Movement-related campaigns—segregation in Cleveland and police violence in Cincinnati come to mind—that are perceived as unfinished business. Simply put, when it comes to commemorating the Movement's history, place matters.

71. Roadside way-finding aid, Farmville, Prince Edward County, Virginia.

The development of civil rights memorials coincides with, and is partly a result of, a phenomenal rise in heritage tourism among African Americans. Just as the Civil Rights Movement sought to increase opportunities for African Americans, the public commemoration of its history has opened the doors of museums and monuments to them. Significantly, survey research indicates that African-American visitors often shop and stay overnight when visiting heritage sites—a fact that that no doubt influenced Virginia's decision to develop the "Civil Rights in Education Heritage Trail," a self-guided driving tour that, in 2008, featured forty-one sites. The R. R. Moton High School in Farmville—stop number twenty-four on the trail—was the scene of a student walkout in 1951 that eventually became one of several school desegregation cases considered by the Supreme Court in *Brown v. Board of Education* (1954). In response, Prince Edward County officials closed its public schools for a decade to avoid desegregation. The building is presently being restored with funds provided by a grant from Save America's Treasures, a partnership of the National Park Service and the National Trust for Historic Preservation.

72. Charles McLaurin, Ruleville, Mississippi.

The different treatment that sites associated with the Movement receive derives, in part, from the efforts of memorial entrepreneurs. As explained by Gary Fine, images of the past do not arise spontaneously but are produced by those with the will and wherewithal to advance their understanding of the past. For Fine, commemoration is a custodial process in which individuals shape how the public conceives of and interprets the past. Charles McLaurin's stewardship of Fannie Lou Hamer's legacy is a case in point. As a Movement activist, he was instrumental in Hamer's participation. As a part of his continued activism, he makes it a point to take heritage tour groups to visit her grave (see Figure 73). For McLaurin—one of only a handful of Student Nonviolent Coordinating Committee (SNCC) activists who stayed in Mississippi after the 1960s—tending to Hamer's legacy reflects a desire to intervene in the politics of the place, to recall what has happened, and, above all, to make progress on the Movement's unfinished agenda.

73. Grave of Fannie Lou Hamer, Ruleville, Mississippi.

The youngest of twenty children, Fannie Lou Hamer labored in the fields as a child, married a sharecropper, and was sterilized without her consent by a state-sponsored program targeting blacks in Mississippi. In 1962, she was among the first African Americans in Sunflower County, Mississippi, to join SNCC's campaign for voting rights. SNCC was at the forefront of efforts to cultivate grassroots democratic change, foment opposition to white supremacy, and foster black empowerment. For her efforts, Hamer was the victim of many violent attacks, including one in which, upon her return to Mississippi from a voting rights meeting in South Carolina, she was savagely beaten by the police. Despite this violence, Hamer remained deeply involved in the Movement, lending to it her passion for rousing hymns, folk humor, and blistering scrutiny of racial politics in America. She acted as the public face of the Mississippi Freedom Democratic Party during its failed bid to seat delegates at the Democratic Party's national convention in Atlantic City in 1964. She would later visit Africa, become the subject of several biographies, and continue to agitate for jobs, education, and votes for African Americans. The restrained, classical lines of Hamer's headstone stand in contrast to her robust, straight-talking style, the gist of which is conveyed by her signature line, "I am sick and tired of being sick and tired."

74. Southern Poverty Law Center headquarters, Montgomery, Alabama.

Clad in brushed steel, its landscaping concretized to deter truck bombs, and a full complement of security personnel guarding its perimeter, the style of the Southern Poverty Law Center's headquarters building offers a sad memorial to the price of civil rights activism in the wake of the Civil Rights Movement. As a matter of fact, the building has been the target of multiple bombs, bullets, and violent protests.

75. Viola Liuzzo memorial, US 80, Lowndes County, Alabama.

Viola Liuzzo, a civil rights activist from Detroit, was murdered by Ku Klux Klan members after she and fellow activist Leroy Moton drove carloads of marchers home following the 1965 Selma to Montgomery march. The iron fence and floodlights at the memorial to Viola Liuzzo suggest the extent to which promoters have tried to deter the vandals who regularly deface it with bullet shots and spray paint. Though speaking in a different context, a resident of Selma, Alabama, aptly summarized the situation: "These heritage guys are basically saying what a lot of people around here feel: The fight goes on. The war never really ends"—a point to which the fences, lights, and guards attest. While civil rights activists carried the day in the 1950s and 60s, to what extent are they winning the battle over the Movement's legacy?

76. Historical plaque, Beale Street, Memphis, Tennessee.

The tension between commercialism and commemoration can undermine the integrity of public history, as illustrated in the challenges of commemorating civil rights history amidst Beale Street's revitalized honky-tonk.

77. Family reunion, Birmingham Civil Rights Institute, Birmingham, Alabama.

In many cases, African Americans visit civil rights sites and memorials as part of a family reunion, offering an opportunity to take part in a tourism destination that recognizes their impact on American history and the site's importance as a cultural attraction. Note the Census Bureau information table in the photograph's lower right corner: the museum was judged a good place to promote Census 2000 to a historically underrepresented group. Will the same be said when it comes time for Census 2050? Will visitors, an ever increasing number of whom have no immediate connection to the Civil Rights Movement, consider these memorials relevant to their daily lives? This is a question confronting civil rights memorial entrepreneurs. The visitors voicing the most critical opinions of these museums are almost uniformly under twenty-five. As one youthful visitor put it in his summary of a civil rights museum's irrelevance to him: "Where's Tupac?" This reference to slain rap artist Tupac Shakur is a not-so-subtle reminder of the growing generational gap between younger and older civil rights partisans.

78. Photo opportunity in Kelly Ingram Park, Birmingham, Alabama.

Smiling tourists who pose for a photo seem strangely out of place against a historical setting of state terror, with a contemporary group of black men looking on in the foreground amongst the statuary of water canons from Bull Conner's memorable stand against Civil Rights protestors in 1963 (see Figures 30, 31, and 35). Significantly, tourists often shop and stay overnight when visiting heritage sites. This fact, combined with the positive publicity that civil rights memorials generate, has persuaded many Chambers of Commerce to support an unabashedly heroic recounting of the Civil Rights Movement. Scenes such as this from Birmingham, however, lend credence to the complaint that there is a conflict between the dignified presentation of public history and the tourism industry's need to promote consumption. Heritage tourism, in its bid to offer something for everyone, risks trivializing the history it commemorates.

Chapter One
Stories Told, Stories Silenced

Standing as Part of, and Apart from, Tradition

The making of memorials, such as Birmingham's Kelly Ingram Park and Chattanooga's King Street, mark points of both longstanding *continuity* and remarkable *change* to the cultural landscape. Civil rights memorials are an expression of *continuity* in that they stand at the head of an enduring tradition of African Americans telling *their* history of America; African-American communities have long commemorated—via whatever means were at hand—an insurgent history of racism and resistance, turmoil and transcendence. But the arrival of the Civil Rights Movement on the cultural landscape also suggests a radical departure from the racist traditions of the past; that is, African-American history is now publicly acknowledged as worthy of commemoration. Along the way to prominence, however, some stories associated with the Movement have been highlighted at the expense of others. This tension between remembering and forgetting harkens back to tensions that characterized the Movement itself, as some campaigns and leaders received more visibility than others. Today, these tensions are inscribed into the cultural landscape.

Traditionally, American public history reflected the hopes and plans of elite, white men. African Americans and the challenge they represented to white hegemony were either marginalized through minstrelsy and tales of happy slaves or barred altogether from the cultural landscape. For instance, the Civil War's memorial legacy largely ignores the role played by African Americans. The handful of monuments from this period that focus on African Americans portray them in the diminutive vis-à-vis whites: following their white officers into battle or on bent knee before Abraham Lincoln in thanks for their freedom. There are even a few memorials in the South to "loyal" slaves who served the Confederacy during the Civil War. Cast as such, the outright absence or the dismissive presence of African Americans served as potent propaganda for the white version of American history.[1]

To the extent they were able, African Americans did not allow this propaganda to go unchallenged. From their earliest arrival in North America, African Americans used stories, songs, and sermons to preserve tales of freedom and bondage, memories of slave uprisings and "bad men" who hewed their own path in the world, and lamentations over trial and tribulation. Out of necessity they nurtured an alternative to the dominant white history. For instance, Lexington, Kentucky's courthouse lawn celebrates the exploits of the Confederate cavalry officer John Hunt Morgan. In contrast, African Americans have long memorialized the site among themselves as the location of the nation's largest trans-Appalachian slave market.

In those instances in which blacks exercised control over their own communal institutions—for example, in the segregated cities of the late nineteenth and early twentieth centuries—they dedicated public buildings and parks to the memory of African-American heroes, such as Crispus Attucks High School and Frederick Douglass Park. In his recent book *The Southern Past*, historian Fitzhugh Brundage discusses the importance of Emancipation Day festivities as a means of instilling a sense of collective memory and identity among African Americans in the post-bellum era. These celebrations, according to Brundage, "had a unique capacity to involve the breadth of the black community, from the college-trained preacher to the illiterate day laborer, from the battle-scarred veteran to the impressionable schoolchild."[2] Collectively, African Americans put forward alternative histories, ones that disputed racist beliefs, such as the happy slave, or that blacks had contributed nothing to American history. As many anti-apartheid activists in the context of South Africa observed, "Ours is the struggle of remembering against forgetting." For African Americans, remembering both injustice and better times was vital to maintaining a sense of identity and purpose. Placed in this broader context, the insurgent narratives etched in stone and steel at civil rights memorials stand as *a part of* a storied tradition of speaking truth to power.

It is no less true, however, to note that recent efforts to commemorate the Movement stand *apart from* this tradition, inasmuch as African Americans now proclaim in public what formerly could only be made known in private. The statuary and symbolism of Kelly Ingram Park are exceptionally powerful in part because they boldly decry racism in what had been a whites-only "public" space. As such, civil rights memorials are different from earlier examples of African-American commemoration. While vibrant and of central importance to African-American communities, older memorial practices were largely confined to the community's private and semi-public spaces. And when the black community occupied city streets and parks to celebrate holidays, such as Juneteenth or the birthdays of Abraham Lincoln and Frederick Douglass, it had only temporary use of these public spaces before they reverted back to white control.[3] Today's civil rights memorials mark a radical break with those past practices by extending a vigorous and authoritative challenge to white supremacy on the cultural landscape. Civil rights memorials have successfully claimed public spaces of commemoration denied to them in the past. Generations of earlier protests strongly condemned racism, but they rarely received official sanction or publicity. Civil rights memorials, with few exceptions, enjoy both. The geography of commemoration— where these stories could and could not be told—has undergone a dramatic restructuring.

Part of the significance of the public portrayal of a version of the past that does not belittle or dismiss African-American experiences lies in recalling the point that a memorial erected in public space must exceed a higher threshold of approval, governmental and otherwise, than other forms of commemoration. As such, a public memorial is a very demanding kind of media, inasmuch as it cannot simply be purchased and installed. Thus, in addition to their compelling statuary and historical significance, the fact that civil rights memorials commonly receive funding from governments and corporations testifies to the power that African-American history commands in the wake of the Movement.

Narrating the Movement, Part One: The Won Cause

Some critics of America's built environment consider grand facades and monuments to be hollow, sentimentalized renderings of what people *wish* the past had been. In their opinion, memorials hide uncomfortable truths behind platitudes and puffery. In many ways, civil rights memorials contradict these critics. Returning to Kelly Ingram Park, the confrontational bearing of the statuary works to dispel the myth that African Americans were happy with their lot and that "outside agitators" were responsible for disturbing the otherwise tranquil state of race relations. With the creation of such memorials, the public portrayal of history in the United States has never been more inclusive of such a distinctly

African-American perspective. That said, critics' skepticism of memorials should not be entirely dismissed. Their concern regarding what memorials simultaneously reveal and obscure raises questions: If it is indeed the case that history is written by the winners, which stories have they included at civil rights memorials? Which ones have they excluded?

The matter of inclusion and exclusion raises a point made earlier: civil rights memorials do not simply present an already available history of the Movement; rather, the version they *re-present* is subject to choices, ones that in contemporary American society are freighted with emotion and political implication. There are two competing perspectives of how to represent the Movement on the cultural landscape. Glenn Eskew, a historian of the American South, refers to the first perspective as the "Won Cause" version of the Movement.[4] Told in contrast to the Lost Cause of the Confederacy, the Won Cause represents the Movement as a story of sweeping cultural and political triumph. Typically, the Won Cause condenses the Movement in time and space to a well-defined era—the fourteen-year period between the Supreme Court's *Brown v. Board of Education* decision in 1954 and King's assassination in 1968—in pursuit of a single goal: integration across the South. By this retelling, heroic leaders orchestrated a regional movement to overcome racist violence and official malfeasance. This interpretive framework predominates at civil rights memorials. It emphasizes elite-led institutions (such as the NAACP and SCLC) and portrays the Movement as a series of key moments (such as the Montgomery Bus Boycott, and the March on Washington) that shifted the balance of power between a progressive vanguard and those seeking to maintain white supremacy. The Won Cause retelling is characterized by a sense of inevitability as the Movement transforms the South at seemingly preordained times and places (Little Rock, Greensboro, Montgomery, Birmingham, and Selma). Importantly, the narrative's *leitmotif* alternates between moods of elation (such as Voting Rights March of 1965) and tragedy (such as the assassination of Martin Luther King, Jr.).

Civil rights memorials are not alone in telling history from the perspective of leaders and elite organizations. The phenomenon—teasingly referred to as the "Great Man" style of retelling history—characterizes most of America's public history sites. American memorials tend to aggrandize leaders, heroes, and national organizations rather than grassroots organizers and local participants. As a result, the contributions of women, workers, and youth are commonly overlooked. The treatment of the life and career of Martin Luther King, Jr. on the cultural landscape reflects the pervasive influence of the Great Man framework. The widespread naming of streets for King demonstrates the extent to which his name has become a popular metonym for the entire Movement. It is not uncommon for communities to link their local struggle for civil rights with King's legacy. Proposals to name or rename roads elicit stories of local activists who marched with King, heard him speak, or simply met him. Street-renaming ceremonies frequently coincide with holiday observances in January or they are held on the anniversary of King's visit to the city. Even the absence of a historical connection with King does not prevent communities from placing him at the center of their Movement commemoration. A stone monument along Pawley's Island, South Carolina's King Street captures this sought-out association well. The monument's inscription reads, "Honoring a world citizen [King] who never walked this road but whose lifeworks helped all of those who do."

In addition to the national holiday and hundreds of public places dedicated to his memory, King is honored in Atlanta at his birthplace, church, and crypt; in Birmingham, at the site of his 1963 campaign against segregation; at the Lincoln Monument, the site of his "I Have a Dream" speech delivered during the 1963 March on Washington; in Selma, for his leadership of the Voting Rights March of 1965; at the site of his assassination in Memphis in 1968; and beside the Mall's Reflecting Pool in Washington, D.C. In contrast, few civil rights memorials reference the people who were essential to building King's reputation and the Movement's success. Among the few who are mentioned—typically Ralph Abernathy, Andrew Young, and Jesse Jackson—King's female advisers are rarely included. For instance, the important role of Ella Baker goes largely unrecognized.[5] Active in anti-racist politics for more than fifty years, she was a close adviser to King and a moving force in the development of the Student Nonviolent Coordinating Committee. Similarly, Septima Clark, a pioneer in the creation of the Movement's Freedom Schools—the unglamorous, grassroots base for the Movement's successful voting rights campaigns—is routinely neglected.[6]

In its favor, the Won Cause's version of the past recognizes the critical contributions King made to the Movement: personal courage, devotion to the cause, and a deft sense of strategy. Moreover, it rightfully calls attention to the Movement's achievements.

Nevertheless, the Won Cause's preoccupation with leadership is terribly out of step with both the reality of civil rights activism and the sentiments that animated the Movement itself. Grassroots organizers, union members, local groups, and individual donors laid the groundwork for King's rise to international acclaim. As Ella Baker said of King, he didn't make the Movement, the Movement made him. The relative anonymity of Jo Anne Robinson and E. D. Nixon illustrates this troubling marginalization. Robinson, an English professor at Alabama State University, and Nixon, a union organizer and member of A. Phillip Randolph's Brotherhood of Sleeping Car Porters, were at the core of a group of civil rights activists in Montgomery, Alabama. They were instrumental in organizing the bus boycott and inviting a young, unknown pastor—Martin Luther King, Jr.—to act as the boycott's spokesman. As president of the Montgomery Improvement Association, King directed a virtual army of women who organized and staffed the effort. Among those who offered him counsel were union organizers, pacifists, Pan-Africanists, and socialists. Their stories are absent from civil rights memorials and will soon be lost altogether to old age and death. Ironically, the Won Cause's preference for the extraordinary and spectacular actually narrows our understanding of the Movement by neglecting the authentic details involved in grassroots activism.

The influence of the Great Man framework extends even to the presentation of the Movement's most famous woman, Rosa Parks. Memorials across the nation prominently display the now-iconic photo of Rosa Parks sitting near the front of a Montgomery bus. The image powerfully testifies to her determination, her courage, and, importantly, her respectability. Seated quietly on the bus, her simple dress and calm demeanor suggest an underlying dignity and unpretentious character. The photo achieved iconic status in part because it addressed middle-class—both white and black—anxieties about the propriety of social activism. It is important to recall that civil rights work was widely seen as radical-inspired rabble rousing; calls for "gradualism" and patience enjoyed more support than is popular to admit today. It is not a coincidence that Parks's arrest set the Montgomery Bus Boycott in motion. As pictured on the bus, she is the antithesis of the disreputable "outside" agitator. Prior to Parks, other black women challenged Montgomery's segregation ordinance. All of them, however, possessed qualities that rendered them vulnerable to slander and defamation. As a result, local activists were hesitant to stake their claim on someone whose character could be questioned. Claudette Colvin's case was typical. Strong-willed and eager to fight racism, she nevertheless had not graduated from high school and was a single mother. Parks's arrest struck a chord throughout black Montgomery and, in time, the rest of the United States: If someone of her character is willing to resist, shouldn't I do the same? Suddenly, the nascent Movement had its heroine, and her arrest—the arrest of a decent, hard-working, church-going woman—catalyzed Montgomery's civil rights community.

Few museums follow the lead of Troy State University's Rosa Parks Library, which presents a fuller, more complex portrait of Parks. For instance, the library's interpretive center discusses her role as the local secretary and youth leader of the Montgomery branch of the NAACP. She undertook this work at a time when the organization was being outlawed across the South. Photographs in the library depict Parks's participation in activist training at the Highlander Folk School, an influential labor and civil rights training center in Tennessee. In contrast to the iconic imagery of Parks on the bus, these photographs have a homey, rather ordinary mien. In the context of 1950s America, however, they are quite extraordinary. They show white and black activists methodically plotting Jim Crow's downfall. The photos offer humble testimony to the hard, painstaking work of social change. In contrast to the image of her on the bus, which abstracts Parks from the community that called forth her heroism in the first place, these photos portray a thoughtful activist-organizer immersed in a larger movement. The manner in which Parks is represented—on the bus or at Highlander—influences how audiences understand activism. Confining Parks to her seat on the bus undercuts the potential for future activism by isolating heroic deeds from their nurturing context.

Narrating the Movement, Part Two: One Goal, Many Movements

In response to its shortcomings, critics of the Won Cause champion an approach that strives to initiate a dialogue with and among visitors as to the role of everyday people in bringing about social change. This approach to representing the Movement mirrors the position of Movement-era activists who sought to upend the traditional relationship between leaders and participants. Ella Baker's response to those seeking a more central role for King is emblematic of those who sought to diffuse the Movement's leadership: "My theory is, strong people don't need strong leaders."[7] Both Baker and Septima Clark wanted to establish vibrant local organizations responsive to local conditions and capable of enduring setbacks. To this end, they encouraged King to lead fewer marches and focus more on developing local leaders and organizations. While they did not deny the utility of charismatic leadership, professional cadres, and legislative politics, Baker and Clark believed that the emphasis on media attention, fund raising, and national politics had dangerous consequences. First, these factors inhibited the leadership capabilities and participation of local, working-class, and otherwise marginalized individuals. Second, they accurately predicted that concentrating power in the hands of a few rendered the Movement vulnerable to violence, leadership failures, and fickle public opinion.

Baker and Clark's concerns are reflected in an alternative approach to the retelling of Movement history. This perspective on civil rights history shifts attention away from great leaders and pivotal moments in order to stress that the grassroots struggle for civil rights was an *everyday* activity that involved ordinary people doing extraordinary things. Whereas the Won Cause conceives of the Movement as a single, unified entity under the leadership of King in pursuit of integration, historians like Clayborn Carson interpret the Movement in terms of multiple "black freedom movements" striving to create and sustain African-American identities and communities.[8] This version of civil rights history examines social networks within black communities, differences in class and gender among African Americans, color consciousness, and the role of workers and labor unions in resisting racism. Accordingly, the emphasis shifts from commemorating legislative and judicial campaigns to the activities of local organizations. What emerges is a sense of the importance of local conditions for organizing as well as the ambiguous connections between local activists and national leaders. Challenges to the Great Man framework arise even in the case of place naming, which is perhaps the most widespread expression of King's dominance over the Movement's legacy. For instance, in Grand Rapids, Michigan, a school board member challenged the idea of naming a school for King, calling him a "generic" leader and asserting the importance of recognizing local civil rights leaders who "had a real impact" on the area.[9]

No single memorial is wholly given over to one perspective or the other; rather, a dynamic tension exists between the two as memorials respond to tensions that characterized the Movement itself. A case in point is the Birmingham Civil Rights Institute's treatment of the tension pervading the relationship between Fred Shuttlesworth, the leader of a local civil rights organization, and Martin Luther King, Jr. In particular, Shuttlesworth clashed with King over the aims of protest demonstrations, yet he relied upon King's "star power" to attract national and international attention. The institute's portrayal of this episode has drawn criticism from local activists and churches for focusing too much on the leadership of the Birmingham campaign to the exclusion of the "foot soldiers" of the Movement. Partially in response to these critics, the institute has designed a new gallery that makes available interviews with local activists via interactive workstations in order to include more information from the "regular" people who staffed the Movement.

The National Voting Rights Museum in Selma, Alabama, exemplifies the grittier, more grass-roots perspective on the Movement. The museum commemorates the struggle for voting rights that culminated in the Voting Rights March from Selma to Montgomery in March 1965 and the passage of the landmark Voting Rights Act three months later. The Voting Rights Museum arose out of the efforts of local activists who were troubled that school students were unaware of the voting rights pioneers living in their midst. Further, the local schools and history museum offered no information about the Movement. In response, the activists came together to re-present the voting rights struggle in a way that reflected the experiences of the local women who organized it. Their intention was to celebrate this local history and to have a positive impact on the lives of Selma's youth.

Selma's traditional cultural landscape resembles that of many small cities across the South. Crossing the Edmund Pettus Bridge, named after a local Confederate hero and U.S. senator, the defunct cotton warehouses along the riverfront give way to a downtown shopping district that has remained healthy and viable in the absence of an interstate connection. Along oak-lined streets, many of the city's remaining antebellum homes have been restored as quaint inns boasting extensive gardens and traditional hospitality. The contrast between the derelict riverfront—once a thriving depot for the region's produce—and the well-groomed bed-and-breakfast district bespeaks the rising importance of tourism in this city.

Not surprisingly, the local cemetery includes a Confederate memorial circle, and across town the remains of a Confederate munitions factory are on display. It was the munitions factory that attracted the attention of Sherman's army on its infamous march to the sea. The resulting three-hour skirmish, referred to by boosters as the "Battle of Selma," is annually commemorated by the local Kiwanis Club. Taking place over the course of a week, the event features an encampment of Union and Confederate reenactors, a mock battle, and an evening ball in period garb. Importantly, African-American participation in these events is minimal, limited to the bussing of school children to the battlefield to observe the mock soldiers on parade.

Set amid this traditional context of war and whiteness, the opening of the National Voting Rights Museum in 1992 marked a radical break with the traditional retelling of Selma's past. Appropriately, the museum is housed in an old cotton warehouse near the foot of the Edmund Pettus Bridge, which is infamous for being the site of the "Bloody Sunday" police riot on March 25, 1965. Around the corner from the museum is the Dallas County Courthouse, to which demonstrators marched in an effort to register for the vote. Drawing on the building's history and the heritage of sharecropping in the area, the museum's motto reads, "The hands that picked cotton can pick presidents."

The Voting Rights Museum has a decidedly vernacular air to it, the result of a largely volunteer staff and folk exhibits. One exhibit, "The I Was There Wall," consists of a mirror covered with post-it notes on which participants have scrawled their recollections of the Voting Rights March. "Living History" exhibits, produced by children, celebrate the role played by local activists. Other exhibits preserve the material effects—sweaters, shoes, and plaster-cast imprints of marchers' feet—of activists who marched to Montgomery. Additionally, the museum offers a guided walking and driving tour of Selma. The tour highlights both the past and present condition of African Americans in Selma. Stops include several African-American churches involved in the Movement, as well as the homes of prominent activists. Museum docents also introduce visitors to the importance of the George Washington Carver housing project along nearby King Street. The site of the first meeting of the White Citizens Council is included as well. Tour directors call attention to Selma's ongoing segregation and the continued dominance of the city by an established white elite. The tour's final leg involves walking across the Pettus Bridge in a small-scale reenactment of the Voting Rights March. Guides make it a point to take tour groups to one of several black-owned restaurants in town and encourage participants to stay overnight in Selma. The tour draws a practical equivalence between the town's established history museum—the Old Depot—and historically black areas as sites properly suited for both making and representing history. The overall result is the antithesis of the Won Cause. It collects and represents local knowledge associated with the voting rights struggle and fosters an appreciation of the gritty details of social change.

Challenges to the Won Cause have led to not only a greater recognition of the ordinary, previously nameless figures in the Movement, but also a desire to place the struggle for civil rights within a broader and more critical historical context. This was certainly on the mind of Abigail Jordan, an African-American activist in Savannah, Georgia, who led a decade-long campaign to build a monument commemorating what she called the "invisible story" of the transatlantic slave trade.[10] The city already had a civil rights museum and a street named for King, but Jordan felt that these memorials celebrated specific leaders and did not capture the struggles and achievements of the black community as a whole. More importantly, she argued that Savannah's slave memorial, unlike these other African-American monuments, would not isolate the struggle for racial equality as a moment in time but as part of a larger African-American journey "that began as a forced voyage across the sea and transformed into an undeniable call for freedom."[11] It is an unfinished journey, according to Jordan, and she implores fellow African Americans to recognize its still evolving nature. On this point, she has said: "Don't just lean back and say, 'Oh, we have made it.' Black folk have not arrived as of yet."[12] The bronze and granite monument expresses this fluid connection between past and present by showing a family of four, dressed in contemporary garb, with broken chains at their feet. Its inscription, written by Maya Angelou to describe the inhumanity of the Middle Passage, reads as follows:

> We were stolen, sold, and b[r]ought together from the African continent. We got on the slave ships together. We lay back to belly in the holds of the slave ships in each other's excrement and urine together, sometimes died together, and our lifeless bodies thrown overboard together. Today, we are standing up together, with faith and even some joy.

The monument drew its most intense opposition from two black city officials who preferred a more heroic and upbeat retelling of history. They succeeded in having the final, more uplifting sentence ("Today, we are standing up together, with faith and even some joy."), which Angelou later contributed, appended to the original inscription.

The Preservation of Civil Rights History

The debate over how to remember the Movement also leads to the question of what sorts of places associated with the Movement's history should be preserved. While, for many, the Movement is epitomized by the sweeping grandeur of the March on Washington in 1963, others think of the Movement as taking place in more mundane places. Places deserving preservation by dint of their service in the Movement include churches, Masonic lodges, restaurants, hotels, beauty parlors, and homes. Protest sites include places of public accommodation, such as bus stations, lunch counters, and bowling alleys. Sites of marches and the places in which marchers were detained are also of great interest.

While calls have been made to preserve these local sites, the recent nature of the events and vernacular character of the sites' architecture pose very real difficulties. Robert Weyeneth, a professor of historic preservation at the University of South Carolina and a pioneering scholar in the study of the Movement's built environment, has observed that there are currently no systematic efforts being made by state and local preservation agencies to document and inventory the numerous places associated with the Movement, many of which are not otherwise noteworthy.[13] In addition, many of the places associated with the Movement have been decimated in the wake of desegregation and so-called urban renewal campaigns.

Important sites are also forgotten because the complex networks of social, political, and economic interests that sustained the Movement are sometimes overlooked. Following the lead of the Won Cause, most civil rights memorials portray the Movement as a succession of inevitably victorious campaigns led by King. He is portrayed as transcending everyday places to move between various corridors of power, shuttling between pulpit and street, courtroom and legislative chamber. Little or no mention is made of the private and semi-public spaces of citizenship schools, neighborhoods, small businesses, and homes where activists found sustenance, developed tactics, and built community. For instance, beauty parlors owned by African-Americans were a key link in the Movement's organizing chain. They were often used for small meetings and as clearinghouses for information. Importantly, their owners were somewhat sheltered from white economic retaliation insofar as their clientele was often exclusively black. As a result, owners of the beauty parlors were insulated from white retribution in ways that, for instance, African-American school teachers who depended on white school boards for their salaries were not. Activists therefore encouraged beauticians to get involved in the Movement. Nevertheless, this link in the Movement's network has not been widely acknowledged, and no such salons have been preserved and commemorated. Given that beauty parlors are one of the business types most frequently found on streets named for Martin Luther King, Jr. (almost twice the national average), their preservation represents a significant opportunity to write a richer commemorative narrative about the Movement and its many levels of participation.[14] When places that nurtured and sustained activism are not commemorated, the Movement's legacy is narrowed. These seemingly mundane semi-public and private places are crucial because the stories associated with them allow for a richer understanding of the mechanics of activism. They also celebrate the uncommon valor of ordinary participants in the Movement, thereby making visible the role of women and working-class activists who are otherwise overlooked.

In all fairness, the Movement's everyday people are not entirely ignored by civil rights memorials. In fact, the memorials often rely upon images of the Movement's participants to play an allegorical role confirming King or some other leader's heroic qualities. This echoes the longstanding practice in Western art of using the female form as an allegorical figure.[15] Commonly, when a woman appears in classical painting and sculpture, it is not a reference to an individual but rather an embodiment of some feminized virtue or vice. In the process, the female form allegorically confirms an individual man's character and destiny. Classic examples include Liberty and Nike whose forms represent the virtues of freedom and victory. As depicted on the cultural landscape, the vast majority of the Movement's participants—both men and women—stand in powerful but silent testimony to the actions of the Movement's leaders. Together, these nameless participants fulfill a role similar to that of the allegorical female form of classical Western art. By virtue of their numbers, enthusiasm, and positioning (for example, as a congregation looking to the pulpit or as protestors following their leader), the feminized mass confirms an individual leader's righteousness.

While sites associated with the history of local activists and women's participation are largely ignored or inadvertently destroyed, some important exceptions to this trend are taking place. For example, in Charleston, West Virginia, the home of a local activist, Elizabeth Harden Gilmore, was placed on the National Register of Historic Places to celebrate her successful efforts to desegregate lunch counters. A similar situation is unfolding along US 80 in Alabama, the route of the 1965 Voting Rights March from Selma and Montgomery. The highway was recently designated a "National Historic Route." The National Park Service, local activists, and tourism interests are in the process of considering how the history associated with such a transitory event can best be commemorated. Suggestions include walking tours of the area, interviews with participants, and an interpretive center dedicated to the common marchers who gave the protest its gravity. Sites such as these hold out the potential for radically altering conventional notions of where history takes place and how it should be preserved.

The Role of Tourism Development

The wave of civil rights commemoration presently cresting across the South has not occurred in an economic vacuum removed from the influence of the highly successful heritage tourism industry. For instance, the arguments over which presentation style best represents civil rights history—the one sweeping and fabulous, the other contextual and mundane—are influenced by heritage tourism professionals who develop and promote historical sites. Many heritage tourism professionals believe that the Won Cause, with its emphasis upon individual greatness and dramatic events, is required in order to attract visitors in an entertainment market saturated with the spectacular and hyper-real. Yet museum docents remark that one of the most common questions from visitors reflects a desire to touch the authentic past: "Is this what it was really like?" The implication is that the opportunity to view authentic artifacts rather than hyper-real recreations motivates many visitors to attend civil rights sites. This desire for authenticity prompts visitors to look for sites with relics that promote a tangible, unmediated encounter with the past, however untenable such an experience may be.[16] Taken to extremes, some civil rights tourists discount popular sites, deeming them to be excessively hyped and simplified. In response, they seek out rare, marginalized experiences—the personal effects of protestors and forgotten sites being especially popular—that they believe have not yet been "soiled" by the heavy hand of public history. While some tourists will find these pilgrimages deeply rewarding, others will despair that, despite their best efforts, the "real" past remains beyond reach, irretrievably lost to the vagaries of "progress." Others, upon reflection, will concede that the very idea of an authentic experience of the past is suspect, the stuff of fabrication and historical fiction. They know that their gaze is an expression of the intellectual milieu in which it developed.

The development of civil rights memorials coincides with, and is in part a result of, a phenomenal rise in heritage tourism among African Americans. This contrasts sharply with the previous absence of attention paid to blacks by the tourism and museum industries. Just as the Movement sought to increase opportunities for African Americans, the public commemoration of its history has opened the doors of museums and monuments to African Americans, inviting them into places that heretofore were the domain of white elites. Memorials to the Movement offer African Americans an opportunity to take part in a tourism destination that recognizes their impact on American history. Further, African-Americans often visit sites associated with the Movement as part of a family reunion, highlighting the welcome afforded them and suggestive of the sites' relative importance among cultural attractions. Significantly, survey research indicates that African-American visitors often shop and stay overnight when visiting heritage sites—a fact that has persuaded many Chambers of Commerce to support the creation of civil rights memorials across the South.[17] The combination of these factors—economic development and positive publicity—suggests why states across the South promote an unabashedly heroic recounting of the Movement only a generation removed from public calls for massive resistance to integration.

Critics complain that the political and financial expediency of the heritage tourism industry compromises the representations of history at memorial sites. The Birmingham Civil Rights Institute offers one example. Birmingham's corporate community gave considerable support to the institute in the hope that it would help address the city's poor image. Toward this end, the museum presents the demonstrations as instrumental in launching a national and, eventually, worldwide struggle for human rights. Designed by American History Workshop, a professional producer of museum exhibits, the exhibit plan was accepted in full by the museum's board, except for the proposed final gallery. In the original plan, the final exhibit was to present a frank assessment of the achievements and shortcomings of the 1963 protests, among which are de facto segregation, continued unemployment, and police violence, all matters that remain problems for Birmingham's black working class. The museum board, dominated by members closely associated with the mayor's office and corporate community, rejected the proposal and instead installed a chronological listing of electoral victories by African-American candidates without any mention of their policies or ongoing challenges.[18] In addition, the board added an exhibit dealing with international human rights. In it the Birmingham protests are cited as a precursor to transnational efforts to increase access to free speech, freedom of religion, and the end of political violence and torture. References to Amnesty International and to the United Nations abound, in the process identifying the international arena as the Movement's next frontier. One implication of this global focus is that Birmingham is choosing to look abroad rather than locally for future progress.

This expansive view of Birmingham's role in the Movement leapfrogs over current local problems to focus instead on creating a better future on a worldwide scale. The same is true of many of the largest civil rights museums. Treatment of contemporary racism and racial politics in the United States is conspicuously absent. Portrayals of racism at these sites focus on white supremacy's most violent and widely scorned expressions: segregation, lynching, and the terrorist group, the Ku Klux Klan. Missing is a sustained treatment of the more mundane and insidious forms of racism that valorize whiteness over other racial identities. Indeed, visitor surveys indicate that most memorials fail to make convincing connections to the present condition of racism here at home. Visitors want to know more about attacks on affirmative action, police surveillance, and discriminatory loan policies. Also, by casting acts of virulent racism as the sine qua non of the segregated order, these museums confirm the popular understanding of racism as an individual pathology grounded in unreasoning prejudice, the effect of which is to displace consideration of racism's institutional and intellectual manifestations.

This absence of a sustained treatment of contemporary racism is particularly apparent when contrasted with the rich historical contextualization of the Movement's origins offered at major civil rights museums. Resistance to slavery, Reconstruction-era politics, and the reign of Jim Crow are variously cited as antecedents and precursors to the Movement and are depicted in considerable detail. One reason for the focus on these events in the distant past along with the hope for the future is that the local present is often too controversial for museums to handle. Interviews conducted with curators and historians at memorials in Birmingham and Memphis suggest that the financial dependency of these institutions on local government and on corporate and philanthropic donors limits the degree to which they can take on issues of contemporary racism. Although these museums are lauded in national and international venues, their funding can easily be threatened by local controversy. This situation suggests that a focus on the national, general, and otherwise distant past is "safe," whereas sustained treatment of the local, specific, and contemporary is not. Thus, in a complex and ambiguous manner, these museums obscure as much about contemporary local racism as they portray about its past. This situation renders the memorials vulnerable to becoming mere repositories of a history that, while powerfully decrying the racism of the past and promoting international human rights into the future, fail to reflect on current events closer to home.

As fiftieth anniversaries of the seminal events of the 1950s occur and as those of the 60s approach, will visitors, an ever increasing number of whom have no immediate connection to the Movement, consider civil rights memorials relevant to their daily lives? This is a question confronting the civil rights memorial landscape. It is worth noting that, among visitors to civil rights museums, the largest differences of opinion are not between men and women or blacks and whites, but between young and old. The visitors voicing the most critical opinions of these museums are almost uniformly under twenty-five. As one youthful visitor put it in his summary of a civil rights museum's irrelevance to him: "Where's Tupac?"—a reference to slain rap artist Tupac Shakur and a not-so-subtle reminder of the growing generation gap between younger and older civil rights partisans.[19]

As mentioned earlier, visitor reactions suggest a highly elastic chronological bounding of the Movement. Many visitors refuse to segment history into neat, chronologically tidy period; rather, they view events in the past as linked to both previous and subsequent events (for instance, the Movement is not a distinct period as much as it is an integral part of a centuries long struggle by Africans for freedom in America). Likewise, the same surveys indicated an interest in learning more about related freedom movements (for women, Chicanos, and American Indians, for example); for these visitors, the Movement is a work-in-progress rather than a completed program—a challenge to the Won Cause rendering of the past.

It would be inappropriate, however, to dismiss civil rights memorials, *prima facie*, as irrelevant or corrupt due to the influence of state and corporate promotion; rather, it is more productive to view their activities within a broader context that appreciates the economics and politics of heritage tourism (a point that will be elaborated upon further in the next chapter). For now, the King National Historic Site in Atlanta's Sweet Auburn District is an instructive example of what can happen when politics and economics encourage the government to rally behind memorial sites. Initiated by Coretta Scott King in 1971 and managed by the National Park Service since 1980, the site had been strapped by budgetary constraints and, until recently, consisted of little more than a small visitor's kiosk on an empty lot adjacent to Dr. King's grave and birthplace. Despite these limitations, the site was attracting more than one million visitors annually. Then, with Atlanta's successful bid to host the 1996 Summer Olympics, officials were confronted by the specter of international visitors arriving in Atlanta to seek out the legacy of the famous Nobel Peace Prize winner and finding only a small kiosk. The situation was reminiscent of the 1950s and 1960s, when the threat of international embarrassment over the condition of civil rights in the United States led the federal government to lend its grudging support to the Movement. In Atlanta, previously uncooperative authorities at the federal, state, and local levels appropriated funds for the construction of a multi-million-dollar visitor center and the restoration of King's childhood neighborhood. The result: the replacement of an empty gesture—a penniless historic site—with an impressive and thought-provoking memorial landscape.

While civil rights museums and historic districts are seen as good for business, some memorials to the Movement are interpreted as economic threats, such as the renaming of streets for King. As we discuss, the most vocal opponents to naming streets for the civil rights leader are typically business and property owners who balk at the cost of changing their address. The opposition of commercial interests often limits how and where King is commemorated in cities, further illustrating how the project of remembering the Movement cannot be divorced from its contemporary economic context. It is difficult to determine what role (if any) a street name plays in generating tourist revenue and other economic development, and it is perhaps this fact that has kept street naming in honor of Dr. King from being fully supported by commercial interests. Even in Atlanta, many businesses resisted the proposal to rename a major thoroughfare for King. Ironically, the successfully renamed street is now the location of significant development and a major landmark in the city's tourism industry. In supporting the street-renaming proposal in 1976, white city council member Wyche Fowler, later to become a U.S. Senator, offered a powerful counterargument to the issue of short-term costs associated with address changes. Fowler contended that a proper recognition of King, "whose name is recognized all over the world," would support Atlanta's desire to develop an "international reputation."[20] In effect, the city that twenty years later would host the Summer Olympics couldn't afford not to commemorate King.

The Role of Protest

While it is true that civil rights memorials often serve local economic development efforts even as they retell the story of the Movement, it would be short-sighted to draw any hard and fast conclusions concerning the impact of this connection on the authenticity and relevance of these sites. To wit, activists often and, in some cases, continually make memorials the site of their own protests. The number and variety of groups protesting at civil rights memorials suggests both the memorials' political relevance and the high degree of indeterminacy surrounding the Movement's contemporary meaning. The King National Historic Site is a case in point. In 1985, the Ku Klux Klan staged a rally at the site to protest what they described as the "corruption" of King's message of equality by the "anti-white" policy of affirmative action. In another instance, African Americans living in the vicinity of King's birth home within the National Historic District in Atlanta protested the proposed renaming of a street in honor of Mahatma Gandhi, claiming that it would detract attention from King and the historic Auburn Avenue neighborhood in which they resided. In a related incident, expatriate Pakistanis protested the installation of a statue of Gandhi near the museum, claiming that Gandhi, as a member of the British army in colonial South Africa, was complicit in the massacre of Zulus and was thereby an inappropriate figure to commemorate at the King National Historic Site. In the summer of 2000, protesters of the verdict of acquittal in New York's *Diallo* police brutality case, in which an unarmed West African immigrant was killed by New York City police, used the site as a stage for their demonstration.

Selma's National Voting Rights Museum also attracts a wide array of political actors. Presidents, vice presidents, and candidates who aspire to those offices have attended the museum's "Bridge Crossing Jubilee." In another instance, approximately forty members of a youth group from Birmingham, "The Malcolm X Grassroots Movement," disrupted a speech by Jesse Jackson on the responsibilities of fatherhood (!) with chants of "No Justice, No Peace." The group complained that Jackson's message and tactics were out of step with the demands of the present and called for a more militant response to racism. The National Civil Rights Museum in Memphis played host to a gathering of local neo-conservatives intent on "reinventing" public housing. In another instance, a group of local prison activists began their march to the city jail from the museum in order to militate against the "legal lynching" of black men.

The impulse to protest finds perhaps its most robust expression in the lone vigil of a Memphis poverty rights activist, Jacqueline Smith.[21] Stationed on an old couch across the street from the National Civil Rights Museum, she has been protesting continuously since the late 1980s, when the Lorraine Motel closed its doors to make way for the museum. Smith lived and worked in the motel until then, and she would often show visitors the room where King spent his last night. Smith's protest is based on her belief that the museum shames King's memory. On a daily basis she rails against conventional notions of commemoration (that a museum is the proper place for history), arguing that the most fitting memorial to King's legacy would be the creation of institutions that support the ongoing struggle for increased access to democratic rights and economic goods and services. A sign at her encampment succinctly expresses her sentiments:

What Jacqueline Smith believes is that the Lorraine Motel should be put to better use such as housing, job training, free college, clinic, or other services for the poor. She also believes that the area surrounding the Lorraine should be rejuvenated and made decent and kept affordable and not gentrified with expensive condominiums that price the poor people out of their community.

Another hand-lettered sign expresses Smith's opinion that the museum is a "9 MILLION $ TOURIST TRAP SCAM" that promulgates hatred and celebrates violence. She blames the museum for "glorifying" the death of King, and claims that the Ku Klux Klan has targeted Memphis for resurgence after seeing its robes and images on display in the museum.

In a sense, Smith has become an exhibit unto herself. Not only is her presence and her protest viewed by nearly all who come to the museum, but she also offers visitors a table filled with photos of King, copies of his books and speeches, and albums of photos, articles, letters, and other comments reacting to her vigil. She displays a list of all those she has convinced not to enter the museum. She has even garnered enough attention over the years to be featured in newspapers and magazines. The power of her protest is attested to by one visitor who wrote, "I almost didn't come in after talking to the woman who lives across the street. While I certainly believe she has a right to have her say, it would be nice to have someone out there to give the opposing view for the city."

Smith plays a dual role in relation to the museum. On the one hand, she is a living testimony to the non-violent protest and tenacity that characterized the Civil Rights Movement and that is depicted within the museum. On the other hand, her continuing anger and discontent belies the apparent finality of the civil rights drama, culminating in the mournfulness surrounding King's assassination as told by the museum. As Bernard Armada has observed, the emotional climax of rooms 306 and 307 is jarred by the view of Smith's vigil that one has through the balcony where King was shot, bringing the visitor sharply back into the present rather than allowing any lingering over the fallen hero.

Published interviews with Smith indicate that her vigil is prompted by deep-seated sentiments rather than a thirst for attention.[22] She does not make her home on the sidewalk because she has nowhere else to go. She has family and friends in the area but chooses her protest space over the comfort of their homes. For the most part, the museum administration respects her space and her right to protest, taking no overt actions against her. For instance, museum administrators, in preparation for an expansion of the museum, included Smith's couch in the project's blueprints, and the board president indicated that she was free to remain as long as she chose. With a restraining order firmly in place that bars her from shouting at visitors, the museum's administration is content to allow her protest, and the free publicity it generates, to continue. There she remains today.

Through the act of interpretation, memorial landscapes—ranging from Chattanooga's now-prosaic King Street to Birmingham's grandiose Kelly Ingram Park—function as a powerful public address system through which activists express their own ideals. Past and future intertwine as a memorial is interpreted and acted upon. On the one hand, then, memorials tend to narrow the story of the Movement in order to emphasize favorable events or perspectives. This is done in part to ensure the support of donors and politicians. On the other hand, as both site and conduit of politics, these memorials act as springboards for a variety of statements. Despite their mainstreaming tendencies, the civil rights memorials do not settle the meaning of the Movement once and for all. Ironically, they can create the opportunity for new struggles over the Movement's meaning.

Conclusion

Civil rights memorials correct the implicit bias present in most American memorials. Typically, African Americans were simply ignored; when they were present, they were included in order to testify to the superiority of whites. Civil rights memorials dismantle this legacy, at once calling shame upon it and contradicting its claims. In a sense, these memorials are an extension of the Movement itself: activists struggled to "desegregate" history books as well as polling booths and public places. Civil rights activists sought to contradict a polarized version of history that cast African Americans as either docile or disorderly and America as the best of all possible worlds. Their revolution extends to the cultural landscape. In concert with public history's growing concern with the lives of ordinary people, these memorials embody the possibility of moving American public history away from its obsession with elite individuals and their homes and toward the remembrance of more mundane, socially representative lives and places. In essence, it is a movement against the version of history that underwrote white supremacy toward one that celebrates its downfall.

Nevertheless, there are significant contradictions and exclusions in how the civil rights era is portrayed. Museums and monuments are major heritage attractions, and the tourism industry is responsible in part for their development and promotion. This influence on memory's landscape requires careful consideration. Additionally, at the nation's largest civil rights memorials, there is a growing consensus as to what the Movement stood for and who its protagonists were. This mainstream narrative forces women's, working-class, and local histories to the margins of the story in order to focus on charismatic leaders and dramatic events. In effect, seeing the Movement as the result of larger-than-life heroes and impersonal forces of history discourages ordinary people from pursuing social change today. Further, in its treatment of racism, the Won Cause rendition of the Movement presents a simplified image that, while compelling in its brutal honesty, nevertheless overlooks contemporary racism's other insidious elements.

The meaning of "civil rights"—how they are achieved, their current status, and their future promise—is currently up for debate on the cultural landscape. In this chapter, we described the ways that civil rights history is being retold and discussed some of the implications of telling the story in this manner. In the process of overthrowing conventions regarding whose history should be remembered and how that history should be commemorated, these memorials reinforce certain traditional notions of who in America makes history. That said, the challenge presented by civil rights memorials has not been confined simply to questions of whose story is and is not shared. The challenge involves where the story is told as well.

Chapter Two
Civil Rights Memorials: How Did They Come to Be?

The production of memorials dedicated to the Movement is a watershed event in the commemoration of American history. The contributions of African Americans to American history were largely neglected prior to the 1970s, with the significant exception of the various Frederick Douglass high schools and Dunbar parks that dotted the segregation era's landscape. Since the appearance of King streets, the historic invisibility of African Americans on the cultural landscape has been redressed—a situation that is impossible to conceive of without the broad political and social change ushered in by the Movement. The result is an intricately woven cultural landscape of museums, parks, plaques, streets, and the like. Nevertheless, these memorials do not mark a complete break with past conventions. Ironically, even as elements of the nation's most popular civil rights memorials reinforce traditional ways of representing American public history, women and workers continue to be overshadowed by elite, albeit black, men. Thus, it can be said that, in the Movement's wake, the canon of American public history has been desegregated but not overthrown.

The cultural landscape's ambiguity, however, is not confined to its content alone. With the arrival of African-American history on the cultural landscape, the very places where Americans commemorate their history are changing as well. Across the country, civil rights memorials—ranging from simple historic markers to multi-million dollar museums—are located amid the declining remains of yesterday's segregation-era business districts and neighborhoods. Today, the scars of urban renewal campaigns, suburbanization, and inequality mark these areas. Although the location of memorials in these places is historically consistent, they are nonetheless not located at the traditional core of civic memorial space—City Hall, the Courthouse, or along Main Street.

A greater appreciation of what has and has not changed on the cultural landscape is fostered by examining the creation of two of the most important types of civil rights memorials: streets and museums. Street names and museums mark opposite ends of the commemorative spectrum in terms of the cost of establishing them and their relative numbers; for instance, museums are expensive and relatively rare while street signs are ubiquitous and less expensive, and the points at which their geography converge and diverge say a lot about how the Movement is commemorated. The lessons offered by "where" and "how" civil rights memorials came about lend insight into the broader question regarding what has and has not changed in the Movement's wake.

The Infrastructure of Memory: Street Naming and Renaming

As discussed earlier, the term "memorial" refers to a wide range of media used to commemorate the past. African Americans have sought to commemorate the Civil Rights Movement at a variety of places, but street naming has proven to be especially important to them. Street names have been used to honor not only Dr. King, but also a host of other figures identified with the struggle for equal rights, such as Harriet Tubman (for example, in Camden, Alabama; Hartford, Connecticut; and Winston-Salem, North Carolina), Thurgood Marshall (in Oxnard, California, and Kingstree, South Carolina), Malcolm X (in Coolidge, Arizona; Washington, D.C.; Boston, Massachusetts; Brooklyn and Harlem, New York), and Rosa Parks (in Detroit, Michigan; Daytona Beach, Florida; Montgomery, Alabama; and Cleveland, Ohio).[1] The death of Rosa Parks in 2005 sparked additional proposals to name streets in her honor—from West Jordan, Utah, to Tampa, Florida.[2] One of the most widely publicized of these proposals came from a group of residents in Clayton County, Georgia, which petitioned to honor her by reidentifying Tara Boulevard, named for the fictional plantation home in *Gone With the Wind*. In a county that is increasingly African-American, the proposed change not only celebrates the achievements of Parks, but also challenges the Old South's mentality that has dominated the region for so long. Indeed, as one of the proponents of the road renaming proclaimed, "The wind done gone"—a reference to Alice Randall's controversial retelling of Margaret Mitchell's novel from a slave's perspective.[3]

Civil rights-related place naming is not restricted to streets; it also has affected the identity of parks, hospitals, schools, and other public places. For instance, the school board in New Orleans, Louisiana, engaged in a highly publicized and controversial school-renaming campaign throughout the 1990s. The names of many white historical figures (including the slave-holding first president, George Washington) were removed from schools and replaced with the names of prominent African Americans, including Martin Luther King, Jr.[4] While there are many civil rights leaders with streets and other items of municipal infrastructure named after them, King streets represent the most common and controversial example of this larger pattern of memorialization.[5]

Seventy percent of places with a King street are located in the seven Southern states of Alabama, Florida, Georgia, Louisiana, Mississippi, North Carolina, and Texas. In addition to the concentration of King streets in the South, significant numbers are found in urban centers on the coasts in California and New Jersey; the industrial Midwest of Michigan, Illinois, (northern) Indiana, and Ohio; and the border states of Kentucky and Maryland (see page 9). Although honoring King with a street name occurs most often in the South, journalist Jonathan Tilove notes that the nation's first renamed streets appeared outside the region. In *Along Martin Luther King: Travels on Black America's Main Street*, Tilove explains that, less than four months after King's assassination in 1968, Chicago leaders renamed South Park Way, a major road but one located entirely within the black Southside.[6] The choice of this street rather than one that crossed the entire city was perhaps seen by Mayor Richard Daley—infamous for issuing a shoot-to-kill order in response to the protests and looting after King's murder—as a way of mending the city's image without offending his political base of racially hostile whites. Two black city aldermen temporarily blocked the renaming of South Park Way, calling for the city to do "something bigger," such as renaming the Crosstown expressway.[7] In 1969, African-American residents in the village of Newcomerstown, Ohio—descended from industrial workers brought up from Alabama in the early twentieth century—successfully petitioned to have their small street renamed.[8]

As illustrated in Chicago and Newcomerstown, naming streets for King occurs in a variety of places—from large cities, such as New York, Los Angeles, and Houston, to some of the country's smallest places, such as Pawley's Island, South Carolina (pop. 138), Denton, Georgia (pop. 269), and Cuba, Alabama (pop. 363). One characteristic that sets the South apart from other regions is that streets named for King appear throughout the region's urban hierarchy, in both non-metropolitan and metropolitan areas. The average population size of a place with a King Street is more than 250,000 outside the South and less than 36,000 within the South. More than sixty percent of the South's cities and towns with a King Street have populations of less than 10,000. A strong relationship exists between the likelihood of a city identifying a street with King and the relative size of its black population. On average, for the United States as a whole, African Americans constitute approximately thirty-seven percent of the population in a location with a renamed street. More than a third of the time blacks make up fifty percent or more of the population in places with a Martin Luther King, Jr. Street.

Given this statistical portrait, it is not surprising to find that latter-day civil rights activists are instrumental in street-naming campaigns. Indeed, local chapters of the NAACP (National Association for the Advancement of Colored People) and the SCLC (Southern Christian Leadership Conference), the organization that King directed, have conducted numerous street-naming campaigns along with various black-led community improvement associations and coalitions. Churches also play an important role in the street-naming process—a reflection of King's status as a minister and the ongoing role of black churches as resource and mobilization centers for civil rights. In fact, churches are one of the non-residential establishments most frequently found on King streets.[9] In the case of Metter, Georgia, a local black pastor led the campaign to rename a street for King, and the subsequent dedication ceremony was decidedly religious. The unveiling of Martin Luther King Boulevard in Metter occurred on the Sunday before the 1996 King national holiday, and the dedication service began and ended with prayer and included the singing of church hymns. During the service, those in attendance read a litany of dedications, pledging themselves to the ideals of peace, freedom, and equality. More recently, in 2005, a group of ministerial councils in Newburgh, New York, were successful in having a street renamed for King. At the dedication ceremony, a local pastor sprinkled holy water on the street as the attending crowd joined hands and sang.[10]

Notably, the connection between naming streets and the black church has not always been harmonious. According to historian Taylor Branch, when King was commemorated with a street in Chicago, the pastor of the historic Olivet Baptist Church, Reverend Joseph H. Jackson, spent thousands of dollars to change the church's entrance to a side street rather than have an address identified with King.[11] Jackson, who collided with King over leadership within the National Baptist Convention, was a conservative opponent to the philosophy of civil disobedience and the Chicago Freedom Movement. The two rivals debated each other on a Chicago television program in 1966, revealing not only personal differences, but also larger philosophical and political divides within the Movement, the black church, and the African-American community.[12]

While King streets represent important conduits for African-American expression, there is no consensus on the meaning and importance of commemorating the civil rights leader. These street names—like other forms of public commemoration—can be seen as "memorial arenas" for debating King's legacy in relation to larger issues of race and power in America. As a result, street-renaming proposals are frequently embroiled in tug-of-wars over the authority to decide whose history will be commemorated where. In some instances, citizens have overturned city council decisions to honor King and restored streets to their original names. Jonathan Tilove reports that voters in San Diego, California, and Harrisburg, Pennsylvania, accomplished this in 1987, when they substituted smaller streets for the major routes originally dedicated to King.[13] A similar reversal of street naming would have occurred in Portland, Oregon, had a county circuit judge not intervened and ruled that placing such an initiative on the ballot was illegal.[14] In another instance, city officials in Americus, Georgia, did not rename a portion of US 19 until black community leaders planned a boycott of city businesses. A white fire department official stoked the controversy when he opined that he would support the renaming proposal as long as the other half of the street was named for James Earl Ray, the man convicted of assassinating the civil rights leader.[15] In Dade City, Florida, vandals painted the name "General Robert E. Lee" over nine Martin Luther King, Jr. Boulevard signs, an incident symptomatic of the South's ongoing struggles over identity and memory. In a single year, almost 100 street signs with King's name in Hillsborough County, Florida, were either spray painted, shot at, or pulled completely from their poles.[16]

In some cases, debate over the proper interpretation of King's character and legacy comes to the fore as opposing forces seek to bolster their arguments. In 2005, a school board member in Exeter, Rhode Island, challenged the decision to include Martin Luther King, Jr. Day within the district's Patriotic Holiday Observation Policy. He argued that, while King was admittedly a great man, he could not be considered a "patriot" in the absence of military service and in light of open protest against his government.[17] Similarly, white street-renaming opponents in Chapel Hill, North Carolina, argued that the debate over renaming a major thoroughfare in his honor actually violated King's principles of nonviolent reconciliation and that something less "controversial," such as a small street or park, would be more in keeping with his legacy. Black supporters countered with King's own words: "The ultimate measure of a man is not where he stands in moments of comfort and convenience but where he stands in times of challenge and controversy."[18] These debates over interpreting King are, according to Michael Eric Dyson, part of a larger national amnesia about King's true legacy. According to Dyson, most of America chooses to remember King as the "moral guardian of racial harmony" rather than as a radical challenger of the racial and economic order.[19] In this respect, the politics of street renaming involve more than simply celebrating King's legacy; rather, they mark a heated contest between the political left and right as well as between white and black over the content and interpretation of that legacy.

One of the largest obstacles facing African Americans as they attempt to elevate King's historical reputation through street renaming is the prevailing assumption, particularly among whites, that King's historical relevance is limited to the black community. In Statesboro, Georgia, African Americans failed twice to have a major road identified with King. During one of these efforts, proponents clashed with a local veterans group over the naming of a new perimeter highway. Veterans represented their memorial cause as inclusive of all races and argued that King was irrelevant to whites. Black leaders unsuccessfully countered by asserting the universal importance of King's legacy, including his work on behalf of peace and economic empowerment for whites and blacks.[20]

In response to a narrow interpretation of King's significance, street-renaming proponents often seek out streets that transcend racial boundaries, trying to rename streets that cross racially diverse neighborhoods. On one occasion, doing so involved extraordinary sacrifice. Martin Luther King, Jr. Boulevard in Austin, Texas, is a major east-west artery in the city. Its renaming, which occurred in 1975, drew intense public debate, particularly from the predominantly white western end. City council members would have probably reversed their decision if not for the witness of J. J. Seabrook, the president of Austin's historically black Huston-Tillotson College, who died of a heart attack while pleading with the city council to keep King's name on the entire street, not just the eastern section.[21] It is this potential to touch and connect disparate groups that makes street naming controversial.

Generally, street renaming proponents have struggled to name prominent thoroughfares that link diverse elements of the city. For instance, in Greenville, North Carolina, West 5th Street became Martin Luther King, Jr. Drive in 1999. Originally, African-American leaders wanted all of 5th Street renamed—not just part of it—but residents and business owners on the eastern end strongly opposed the proposal. King's name marks an area with a largely African-American population, whereas East 5th is mostly white. More recent attempts to rename all of 5th Street failed, leading to deep frustration within the city's black community. In the words of one leader, "[t]he accomplishments of Dr. King were important to all Americans. A whole man deserves a whole street."[22] Seeking to settle what they saw as a "divisive" issue, white municipal leaders voted in February 2007 to rename the city's bypass for King and ordered that the existing Martin Luther King, Jr. Drive revert back to West 5th Street. Consequently, a major racial boundary in the city remained unchallenged and African Americans were obligated to change their addresses while whites along East 5th Street were not.

In Brent, Alabama, the civil rights leader would have been honored on a street leading to a city garbage dump if not for the protests of an outspoken black minister.[23] Martin Luther King Circle in Phoenix, Arizona, is a small cul-de-sac adorned with a "dead end" sign. The establishment of a state holiday for King was almost a dead end in Arizona until the state was threatened with tourism boycotts. According to photojournalist Keli Dailey, the Phoenix street is invisible on some city maps, and, until recently, its six homes were owned exclusively by African Americans.[24] Past efforts to rename a larger road have failed. In 1995, a newspaper reporter described Martin Luther King, Jr. Drive in Jackson, Mississippi, as a "Boulevard of Broken Dreams," highlighting the intense poverty, segregation, physical deterioration, and crime found along the road.[25] More recently, in 2004, a federal prosecutor declared that a three-square-mile section centered on Martin Luther King, Jr. Avenue in Knoxville, Tennessee, had contributed more than forty-five percent of gun-related homicides since 1992, making it "the most violent area in the city."[26]

The renaming of depressed and obscure streets after King has led to the stereotype that all King streets are similarly hapless. There are exceptions, such as Tampa, Florida's King Street, which runs more than fourteen miles, connects with two interstate highways, and serves as home to more than 500 non-residential and business addresses.[27] King's namesake in Des Moines, Iowa, was proclaimed by the local newspaper to be the "strongest street in town," because of its low crime rate, increasing home sales, and numerous renovation and construction projects.[28] While King streets present a complex picture that cannot be reduced to a single image, preliminary census research supports the popular perception that these named roads are typically located in neighborhoods that are poorer and more African-American than citywide averages.[29] Research by geographer Matthew Mitchelson reveals that the majority of the nation's King streets are one mile long or less. Although approximately thirty percent of all King streets stretch one to five miles, few extend beyond five miles. Mitchelson has also examined the type of streets named for King as classified by the U.S. Census. More than eighty-five percent of the time King's name is found on "neighborhood roads," understood to be small, residential streets; the remaining number of streets are split between "primary roads" (such as state and national highways) and "secondary and connecting roads" (such as large roads that feed into highways).[30]

Many street-renaming proponents see the naming of major thoroughfares as a reflection of the importance that a community places on King's legacy. They feel that smaller, less visible streets restrict the public impact of King's image and reinforce boundaries rather than serving as bridges across racial divisions. Realizing this fact, some outspoken African Americans have sought to find King a more central place within America's cities. For instance, in 2001, a local chapter of the NAACP in Clearwater, Florida, called for the removal of King's name from a narrow, three-block street that extended only 500 feet. Its campaign resulted in a rare victory: the renaming of larger road that cuts through a variety of neighborhoods and the city's historically African-American business district.[31] A protester in Arkadelphia, Arkansas, placed garbage bags over two signs that designated the Pine Street Bridge as the Martin Luther King, Jr. Bridge. Chained to one of the covered signs, he argued that the signs were insultingly small and demanded that all of Pine Street be renamed instead of just the bridge.[32] In Muncie, Indiana, public sanitation worker Randall Sims organized a "unity line" of 200 demonstrators in support of renaming Broadway Boulevard for King. For more than twenty years, the civil rights leader's name had been attached to an overpass in Muncie, but Sims was calling for a memorial with a higher profile.[33]

When faced with the choice of naming an inferior street for King or not commemorating him at all, some African Americans have chosen the latter. This was the case in Brookhaven, Mississippi, where a resident of Hamilton Street fought a proposal to rename the street for King, arguing that "it would be a honor to be renamed after him, but the crime, drugs and years of financial neglect by the city board makes it undeserving of his name."[34] The resident also questioned why city leaders chose to rename a black neighborhood street located so far away from the downtown general public and the developing west side of town. African Americans living on Reese Street in Athens, Georgia, opposed identifying their street, which they described as "unknown" and "drug-infested," with a great historical figure.[35]

Finding a prominent place for King proved particularly controversial in Danville, Virginia. In 2001, African-American activist Torrey Dixon petitioned the city council to rename Central Boulevard, a major commercial thoroughfare, in honor of King, who lent his support to a failed effort to desegregate the city in 1963. Dixon chose the street because its high volume of traffic would provide high visibility for King's name. In addition, Central Boulevard crossed the Aiken Bridge, which memorialized a segregationist judge, Archibald M. Aiken, who issued the injunction that led to the arrest of hundreds of civil rights demonstrators in 1963.

Significant public opposition to renaming Central Boulevard arose, and city officials rejected Dixon's request. They suggested renaming High Street, a smaller street serving a predominantly African-American population. Moreover, High Street Baptist Church functioned as a focal point for local civil rights activists when King visited Danville in the 1960s. Dixon rebuked the counterproposal, saying, "I think Dr. King should have a major road named after him. I think having a road in a low-class neighborhood named after King is offensive."[36] Events in Danville illustrate the importance of location in the street-naming process and how the renaming of a less prominent street, even one with a historical association with King, can be viewed as degrading.

Street naming is the most widespread practice in the broader effort to commemorate the Movement. The growing frequency of King streets signals a significant increase in the political power of African Americans. That said, the intra-urban location of most King streets and the contested nature of the naming process prompts questions as to the extent to which civil rights memorials have overturned long-established patterns of segregated commemoration. After visiting dozens of King streets, Tilove emphasized the rich community life that courses through them. Nevertheless, he observed that "to name any street for Martin Luther King, Jr. is to invite an accounting of how that street makes good on King's promise or mocks it."[37] The implicit tension between commemorating the ideals that animated King's vision of the Beloved Community and making good their unfulfilled promise is characteristic of civil rights memorials in general.

Civil Rights Museums

Just as King's memory so thoroughly dominates the naming and renaming of streets, his legacy is front and center when it comes to civil rights museums, the crown jewels among the Movement's memorials. With their carefully designed grounds, statuary, temporary galleries, gift shops, educational outreach programs, and development officers, these museums go far beyond their permanent exhibits to become one-stop memorial malls that try to present something for everyone.

These museums are located primarily in the South. The most significant civil rights museums, in terms of their size and audience, are located in Atlanta, Birmingham, and Memphis and are closely associated with the life and career of Martin Luther King, Jr. A point of contrast is Selma's National Voting Rights Museum. As already discussed, the vernacular style of this museum sets it apart from the highly capitalized, tightly programmed museums found in larger cities. These four museums represent a cross-section of the broader field of civil rights museums: they are characterized by broad similarities and pointed differences in the extent to which they commemorate the Movement, the types of media they employ (ranging from folk collections to high-tech displays), and the political-economic contexts of their operation. Each of these four museums is profiled below in a separate subsection. Given the complex interplay of text and context that characterizes memorials and their environments, investigating the location and establishment of civil rights museums shows that, while the events of the past have already happened, the politics of memory that condition their interpretation serves many, sometimes conflicting, interests in the present.

King National Historic Site, Atlanta, Georgia

The location of the King National Historic Site in Atlanta is symbolic of the complexities that characterize public memory in the South. Several blocks to the west are the skyscrapers of Peachtree Street, the economic vitality of which led some Atlantans to boast that they were "too busy to hate" during the 1960s. A short distance to the east is the Carter Presidential Center, housing the Carter Center and the Jimmy Carter Library. The recently completed Freedom Parkway links the three sites, all of which are closely associated with the New South. At the same time, signs near the King National Historic Site and along the Freedom Parkway direct visitors to Stone Mountain State Park. It was from atop Stone Mountain that the Ku Klux Klan was reborn in 1915. Into its granite face are carved the mounted figures of four Confederate generals. This poignant juxtaposition of iconic elements from the Old South and the New South underscores the site's position astride the fault lines of memory.[38]

In more local terms, the King National Historic Site (KNHS) and its associated National Preservation District are located on Auburn Avenue, the one-time heart of the city's black community. By the middle of the twentieth century, Auburn Avenue's concentration of segregated banks, insurance companies, professionals, and churches earned it the reputation as the wealthiest African-American street in the nation. With the increasing mobility of the 1950s and 1960s, however, came more opportunities to move from Auburn Avenue, and the neighborhood began a slow decline. Many of its businesses and elite residents relocated to the neighborhoods associated with the historically black colleges and universities of Atlanta's West End. Moreover, in the early 1960s, the construction of an interstate bisected the street, effectively severing its residential portion from downtown businesses. By 1970, when King's tomb was moved from Southview Cemetery to grounds near Ebenezer Baptist Church, the neighborhood showed the typical signs of social fragmentation and financial distress.[39]

In contrast to the extensive interpretive presence currently provided by the National

Park Service, the KNHS for nearly fifteen years after its establishment in 1980 consisted of little more than small tours of King's birthplace and Ebenezer Baptist Church. Although willing to commission the site, Congress was unwilling to allocate funds to construct basic facilities, such as an exhibit hall, parking lot, and restrooms. While the KNHS attracted 350,000 visitors in 1984 and by 1991 two million annually, with a small interpretive presence and little to see or do most visitors remained on site for less than thirty minutes. The large number of visitors overwhelmed the site's limited facilities and resulted in numerous inconveniences for the neighborhood's, residents, who were left to fend for themselves. Problems included the diesel fumes from idling tour buses, noise, and intense competition for parking.

Neglect of the KNHS came to an end with Atlanta's successful bid to host the 1996 Centennial Olympic Games. National Park Service personnel deftly used the coming of the Olympics, and the international scrutiny that would accompany the event, to lobby for increased funding. Although international visitors were generally unfamiliar with Atlanta, they were well acquainted with Dr. King's legacy. Further, the paucity of the KNHS contrasted unfavorably with sites associated with the Confederacy and the Old South that dominated Atlanta's established cultural landscape at Stone Mountain and on the grounds of the state capitol. The mismatch between King's international stature and the ramshackle condition of the historic site threatened international embarrassment.

In response to the impending crisis, Georgia's Congressional delegation, the Atlanta Committee for the Olympic Games, and the National Park Service (NPS) initiated intense lobbying efforts in search of funds to improve the site. At the heart of their plan, which totaled nearly $12 million, was the construction of a multimedia visitor center to be built on the site of the existing King Neighborhood Community Center. The mayor's office and the city council agreed to donate the community center and its parcel of land to the KNHS in return for the promise that a new community center would be built in the future with NPS funds. When this plan encountered opposition in Congress, the Georgia delegation confronted the House and Senate with budget figures demonstrating that, even though KNHS was one of the three most visited sites among the NPS's urban parks, exceeded by only Independence Hall in Philadelphia and the Statue of Liberty in New York harbor, it had received less than twenty percent of the funds spent on developing comparable sites. The stark contrast in the figures, which implicitly leveled the charge of racist budgetary practices, persuaded Congress to apportion the necessary funds with the single caveat that none of these appropriated monies would be used to construct a replacement community center. Over a decade later, the NPS's promise to rebuild the community center has yet to be fulfilled, and a site once dedicated to assisting the area's working-class African-American residents now caters to tourists from home and abroad.

A final hurdle to the completion of the proposed changes came in the form of direct opposition to the plan by the King family.[40] After initially supporting the plans for expanding the King National Historic Site, the family, led by Coretta Scott King, withdrew its support from the project when they learned that the visitor center would include an exhibit on King's life and career. In place of the NPS plan, the King family proposed building an interactive, edu-tainment center called "King Dream," modeled after the Universal/MGM Studios venue in Orlando, Florida. The planned facility would depict events from the Movement via holographic and other multimedia exhibits. Proceeds from the venture were pledged to further nonviolent social activism.

In pursuit of its efforts, the King family barred the NPS from conducting tours of the King birth home, called for a halt in construction of the visitor center, and demanded that the NPS abandon all of its activities. In response, the NPS rescinded its $535,000 annual subsidy of the family's King Center for Nonviolent Social Change. Members of the King family and King Center staff argued that the Park Service was stealing the family's legacy and, further, that, as a federal agency, it was not in a position to interpret "people's history." Nonetheless, African-American community leaders, local residents, business owners, representatives of the city council, the mayor, and state and federal representatives continued to back the NPS's plan. Over the years, the family's withdrawal from Auburn Avenue drew unfavorable comparisons with NPS's careful investment in the community's security and appearance. Perhaps most critical in the eventual success of the NPS plan were a series of editorials and opinion columns that appeared in newspapers and magazines across the nation, lambasting the family as greedy. An *Atlanta Journal Constitution* investigation into King Center finances revealed an institution beset by disorganization and improprieties.[41] In the face of such antagonism and lacking any outside source of funding for the proposed facility, the King family withdrew its protest.

Since then, the family has invited the NPS to purchase the King Center property on Auburn Avenue and elsewhere.

The new facilities and tours at the KNHS opened several weeks prior to the beginning of the 1996 Olympic Games. Robert Weyeneth noted that, among the steps taken to introduce the improved site, organizers placed prominent advertisements in the international terminal at Atlanta's Hartsfield Airport. No similar advertisements were placed in the domestic terminal, a significant sign of the disjuncture between international and domestic memorial politics that allowed the site originally to languish.

Birmingham Civil Rights Institute, Birmingham, Alabama[42]

In Alabama, the Birmingham Civil Rights Institute (BCRI) emerged from the efforts of a group of academic and legal professionals who aligned themselves with the city's first black mayor and, more broadly, with the liberal, middle-class coalition that dominated city politics beginning in the late-1970s. The original proposal for BCRI was put forward in 1979 by then-mayor David Vann. As a white liberal, Vann served as a mediator during the 1963 campaign, and he was party to the negotiations that followed the demonstrations. He was elected to city council in 1971 and to the mayor's office in 1975 by a coalition of black and white voters. During his first term, however, Vann's coalition fell apart in the wake of a police shooting of a young black woman and his subsequent refusal to suspend the offending officer. Running behind in the polls with the next election approaching, Vann proposed a civil rights museum. In response, Birmingham's City Council convened a committee to investigate the idea. Vann lost the election, but the winner, Richard Arrington, the city's first black mayor, endorsed the idea of a museum.

Despite a mayoral endorsement, the project suffered for lack of appropriations and stagnated in committee throughout Arrington's first term. This was due in part to opposition from some city council members to funding the museum. Proponents of the museum argued that the city was best known for its civil rights history and that none of the city's existing museums reflected Birmingham's African-American heritage. Further opposition to the museum project stemmed from a general apprehension about examining the past. Running as an unspoken subtext throughout the on-again, off-again deliberations was the tacit wish of many in Birmingham to ignore the past for fear of attracting criticism or exacerbating existing racial tensions. This feeling was pervasive enough that Arrington, who was elected by a narrow margin and whose support among white voters was tenuous, did not push for the museum with much determination.

Arrington won reelection in 1983, as he would do five times over the course of two decades, and the museum project gathered momentum. Importantly, the project received the endorsement of the downtown business association, Operation New Birmingham. Created in the wake of the 1963 demonstrations, Operation New Birmingham brought together many of the city's most powerful corporate magnates, real estate agents, and attorneys for the specific purpose of addressing the city's poor public image and attracting commerce to the central business district. While members of Operation New Birmingham recognized the district's potential for controversy given local opposition and institutional turf wars over limited funding for the arts, they backed the project's potential for improving the city's image and attracting visitors. As was the case in Memphis, discussed below, the twin arguments of a need to rectify the city's image coupled with the promise of tourist revenues helped to secure several million dollars from corporate donors—many of whom had supported the city's segregationist establishment only two decades earlier.

In November 1985, the city allocated funds for the purchase of a half-block parcel of land adjacent to Kelly Ingram Park and Sixteenth Street Baptist Church for the museum. Early in the process, some proponents of the museum lobbied for a parcel closer to the Fourth Avenue business district as a way of improving its sagging fortunes. One white committee member suggested that few people would visit a museum located near Kelly Ingram Park due to that area's reputation as a dangerous part of town. He argued that the museum be placed at a site near the affluent, largely white suburb of Mountain Brook, along the city's border. He also suggested that the name of the museum drop any reference to "civil rights"—considered by many whites to be unduly partisan—and that it be replaced with the term "human rights."[43] Neither of these suggestions was adopted, and the eventual site chosen for the museum received the support of the city council and the museum board as well as the local editorial pages. Pleased proponents described the area around the park and church as a "sacred space" in which the cause of freedom had been forwarded, likening its importance to that of Valley Forge in the nation's democratic experience.

Museum construction commenced in February 1991, but the project remained a controversial issue: the ground-breaking ceremony was protested by black activists who complained that working-class citizens had been left out of the planning process. The opposition prompted the city to hire public relations experts to orchestrate the opening of the BCRI. The consultants gauged public opinion, both locally and nationally. Locally, the fact that two bond issues were voted down by Birmingham's majority black electorate combined with some critical editorial commentary was cause for concern. Nationally, the city was viewed as a hotbed of racism, with its reaction to the planned museum interpreted as yet another indication of widespread bigotry. The consultants decided to counter these opinions by focusing on the message that "Birmingham accepts its past, has begun the process of healing, celebrates its vital role in civil rights history, and continues to make progress toward improved race relations."[44] This idea was the central theme of a campaign that sought to position the BCRI as a tribute to the city's civil progress and as a boon for future development.

The Birmingham Civil Rights Institute opened in 1992. The final cost of the project totaled $12 million, with the majority of funds coming from the city, a portion from Jefferson County, and a $4 million commitment from local corporations. The result is a structure whose design elements echo those of the nearby Sixteenth Street Baptist Church and Kelly Ingram Park. Sitting on adjacent corners at the intersection of Sixteenth Street and Fourth Avenue, the three sites form a coherent whole. Originally, this area lay astride the boundary between white and black commercial districts. Today, in what has become a majority black city surrounded by white suburbs, it sits at the intersection of the Movement's success and failure. Compounded with the difficulty of getting loans, neglect of property by absentee landlords, and suburbanization, the traditional black business district declined. As a result of the dismantling of legal segregation, the black businesses adjacent to the district lost their reason for existence as African-American consumers, integrated with whites under the sign of the dollar, took their business elsewhere. The dilapidated condition of the area around the Civil Rights District contrasts sharply with the relative prosperity of the city's central business district and surrounding suburbs.

That said, with the opening of the BCRI and the revival of the park and church, the largely African-American Fountain Heights neighborhood has become the focal point of competing proposals to revitalize the area.[45] One proposal backed by Operation New Birmingham and local real estate developers calls for the removal of several run-down or abandoned residences to be replaced with upscale shops and townhouses along the lines of a gentrified urban village. The other proposal, put forward by a coalition of Fountain Heights residents, calls on the city to fund new sidewalks, sewer repairs, street lights, and a local police substation. After several confrontational meetings of the city council and a protest march, the two sides reconciled over a proposed settlement. Although the new upscale construction will occur, the city will ensure that the upgrades in infrastructure are extended into the entire neighborhood and not just the part being gentrified. For the time being, however, the Civil Rights District is likely to remain as it is—a landscape memorializing the very Movement that inadvertently contributed to the negative consequences that now define the surrounding neighborhood.

National Civil Rights Museum, Memphis, Tennessee[46]

In Memphis, the National Civil Rights Museum (NCRM) memorializes the site of King's assassination at the Lorraine Motel on April 4, 1968. Immediately following the assassination, the motel's owner, Walter Bailey, working in tandem with the SCLC, marked the site with a plaque. While thousands of tourists and pilgrims visited the motel annually, subsequent efforts to create a more extensive memorial failed. Barely surviving on a customer base undercut by integration and the declining fortunes of small, inner-city motels, and facing the threat of foreclosure and possible demolition in 1982, Bailey recruited a local radio station, WDIA, and a civil rights attorney, D'Army Bailey (no relation), to help him transform the motel into a memorial befitting King's memory. WDIA, the first radio station in the South to feature black disc jockeys, catered to Memphis's African-American community, and it had taken the lead in several high-profile fund-raising efforts. A non-profit foundation was established under D'Army Bailey's leadership. The foundation's board included the president of Memphis-based and black-owned Tri-State Bank, a local member of the state legislature, the president of Memphis's Lucky Heart Cosmetics, and the executive director of the AFSCMEU (American Federation of State, County, and Municipal Employees Union)—the union that emerged from the 1968 strike that Dr. King died supporting.

The foundation acquired the property at a foreclosure auction, thanks to a last-minute loan from Tri-State Bank and donations from the union, the cosmetics company, and the holder of the building's mortgage. In early 1986, bills were introduced into the state legislature on behalf of the project. After a bout of intense lobbying, a deal was struck whereby the state agreed to pay half of the nine million dollars in capital costs, with the city and county accounting for the remainder. Funding for the exhibits and operating costs were raised from local corporations, such as Federal Express and Browning Ferris Industries. The exhibit space portrays major events in the Civil Rights Movement and incorporates portions of the original motel, including the balcony on which King was shot and the room in which he stayed. The museum also emphasizes international human rights by annually recognizing a leader in the field with its Freedom Award (past winners include Nelson Mandela and Yitzhak Rabin). A new wing of the museum—funded entirely by private donations—incorporates the boarding house from which the assassin operated and presents information regarding various theories associated with King's murder.

As with the Birmingham Civil Rights Institute, the NCRM attracted donations and praise from around the country while suffering the criticism of local opponents. Some argued that the site, a mark of civic shame, should be obliterated rather than transformed into a shrine or attraction. Others, fearing a drain on the budgets of already existing cultural institutions in the city, argued that no public funds should be spent on the museum. Finally, some charged that King's legacy would be more appropriately served by the creation of a job training center, homeless shelter, or school rather than a multi-million dollar cultural complex. The most outspoken proponent of this latter position was and is Jacqueline Smith, an activist who protests the museum from a sidewalk encampment several feet from the entrance (the details of her story were presented in Chapter One). Museum supporters argued in return that preservation of the actual site provides an invaluable link to the past, and the city's reputation was at risk in light of the thousands of visitors who annually made their way to the derelict site prior to its refitting.[47]

National Voting Rights Museum, Selma, Alabama[48]

Unlike the museums in Atlanta, Birmingham, and Memphis, the focus of the National Voting Rights Museum (NVRM) in Selma is on the local activists who militated for voting rights during the late 1950s and 1960s. Their activities culminated in the Voting Rights March from Selma to Montgomery in March 1965 and the passage of the Voting Rights Act. In contrast to the museums in Atlanta, Birmingham, and Memphis, the NVRM has no fancy exhibits designed by specialists using state-of-the-art techniques and materials; rather, the display items were donated and the exhibits designed by volunteers. For instance, marchers were asked to stop by the museum to have plaster cast imprints of their feet created. Throughout the museum, the emphasis is on preserving the memory of the homegrown activists who fought for voting rights. The result is a museum that is decidedly local in its focus. This sets it apart from the sweeping scope of the stories told in Atlanta, Birmingham, and Memphis, where the scale of the story embraces the entire nation (sometimes the world) and highlights the impact of leaders such as Dr. King.

Hank and Rose Sanders, Harvard-trained lawyers and civil rights activists, were responsible for the museum's inception. Rose Sanders was especially active in issues related to education, and she played a key leadership role in the boycott of Selma's high school in 1990 following the dismissal of the school district's first black superintendent. She is also the driving force behind a number of youth-oriented leadership and performing arts groups in Selma. At the time of the high school boycott, the couple became aware of a lack of information about the Civil Rights Movement in the local school district's curriculum and the local history museum. The Sanderses were especially troubled that local students had little or no idea that voting rights pioneers were living in their midst. In response, the couple decided to create their own museum.

The National Voting Rights Museum opened in 1992 under the direction of an executive board comprised of both local figures associated with the Movement, students, and nationally known figures, such as Congressman John Lewis of Georgia and Reverend Jesse Jackson, who lent their names to fund-raising efforts. A complicated series of events led to the museum's present location in an old cotton warehouse that had been converted to retail space along the Alabama River in downtown Selma. Before securing this location, the Sanderses and other organizers struggled to find a suitable space for the museum. The difficulty was due in large part to the reluctance of downtown landlords to rent space for a civil rights museum, which many of them considered to be a controversial and divisive project. The present building was obtained after Deans Barber, a white property owner and member of the Dallas County Commission, broke ranks with other downtown landowners over a property dispute and sold his building—an old cotton warehouse near the Edmund Pettus Bridge—to the museum organizers.

Initially, the NVRM relied almost exclusively on private funds and donations for its operation. This has changed over time as public funds and support have come to play an important role in the museum's operation. The bulk of the funding for the purchase of the building and its necessary repairs came from former activists living in the area, the Sanderses, and the law firm in which they are partners. At the urging of the local Visitors Bureau and Chamber of Commerce, the city contributed an annual stipend of between $10,000 and $15,000 to the overall budget and included the museum in its tourism brochures. Additionally, the director of Alabama's Bureau of Travel and Tourism black heritage promotion, Frances Smiley, included the museum in that agency's literature.

Outside marketing and promotional support was important as the museum's budget was too small to support its own marketing campaigns. The majority of operating funds came from visitor donations and the sale of voting rights memorabilia from the museum's gift shop. The composition of the budget, however, began to change in 1994, when Hank Sanders was elected to the Alabama Senate. As chairman of the Finance and Taxation Education Fund, he has overseen state appropriations for education projects. Several of these grants have gone to the NVRM. As a result, state funds made up half of the museum's $300,000 budget in 1997. While the state funds have been of great help to the museum, the city of Selma stopped providing any monies once state funding became available. To assist with further fund-raising, the museum's executive board has extended invitations to nationally recognized individuals, such as attorney Johnnie Cochran and basketball player Shaquille O'Neal. Additionally, the museum has received several thousand dollars in grants from International Paper Corporation, the county's largest employer, for the development of a voting rights curriculum.

The museum's detractors claim that it is a patronage project that promotes disunity and improperly uses state funds. They cite visits by Louis Farrakhan and Kwame Toure (né Stokely Carmichael) as divisive and incendiary. An investigation into a possible conflict of interest between Hank Sanders's involvement with the museum and his oversight of state appropriations concluded with no charges being filed. In another instance, a state representative and rival of Sanders for leadership of Selma's black community charged that the museum illegally used the services of an administrative aide associated with Sanders's office. While nothing came of the charges, the incident and others like it suggest the level of scrutiny and opposition under which the museum operates.

Although the museum suffers at the hands of its critics and from insecure finances (state grants notwithstanding), its impact on the city's economy has been important. The Chamber of Commerce's president recognizes tourism as the city's largest source of income. In its promotion of the past, the city goes to great lengths to represent itself as possessing heritage sites related to both the Civil War and the Civil Rights Movement. Nevertheless, it is the NVRM, with its exhibits and the annual commemoration of the Voting Rights March, which draws the majority of visitors to Selma.

The importance of the museum and civil rights tourism more generally promises to grow with the completion of the Selma to Montgomery Historic Trail. The trail is designated an "All-American Road" by the U.S. Department of Transportation and a "Scenic Byway" by the Federal Highway Administration, and Congress and the Clinton Administration added the fifty-four-mile stretch of US 80 between Selma and Montgomery to the list of the country's National Historic Trails in 1996. Jointly administered by the National Park Service and the Department of Transportation, the project carries with it $3 million in development and implementation funds to be spent in the three counties traversed by the March: Dallas, Lowndes, and Montgomery. Visitor centers, outdoor exhibits, and recreational areas are to be constructed in Selma and Montgomery and along the route of the march. An eighteen-member steering committee includes veterans of the Movement, Park Service representatives, and state and local tourism development officials. Additionally, a Movement-era activist chairs each county's citizen input board.

While Alabama has recently been successful in attracting outside capital investment, the majority of the economic development has been near the state's traditional industrial centers of Birmingham, Huntsville, and Mobile. Relative to those areas, central Alabama has lagged behind. Local boosters hope the US 80 project will prove to be an economic boon to the area. Nevertheless, questions remain as to the extent of the role that the NVRM will play in the project. Proposals under consideration by the museum board range from keeping the museum entirely independent of the National Historic Trail to relocating the museum to a new building several blocks away from its present location and making it into the primary interpretive facility for the trail. The primary concern of the museum's board revolves around the degree of autonomy over historical content and interpretation it would retain if the board accepted federal funding.

Conclusion

Streets and museums offer points of comparison and contrast with regard to civil rights memorials. Streets named for Martin Luther King, Jr. illustrate just how widespread commemoration of the Civil Rights Movement has become. Given the significant cost of establishing and operating a museum, the naming of streets represents a way for African Americans—particularly in small towns and rural areas—to remember and honor the Movement without incurring the significant cost of establishing and operating a museum. This is not to suggest that the location and production of street names and museums are mutually exclusive. In Selma, for example, King's namesake street has been incorporated into a walking tour of civil rights historical sites in the city. The docents of the National Voting Rights Museum promote the tour. Also, the Reverend Ralph Mark Gilbert Civil Rights Museum in Savannah, Georgia, is located on Martin Luther King, Jr. Boulevard. Given that black leaders in Savannah, such as Gilbert, tried to bar King from preaching in the city, this association suggests a connection between national and local civil rights leaders that perhaps never existed.[49] This sort of ambiguity—street signs and museums can share the same place but communicate very different messages about it—sometimes characterizes the location of civil rights memorials.

The politics of street naming and museum creation provide insight into the important role that racial boundaries continue to play in the post-Movement era. Because street signs are seemingly ordinary and lack the ornate qualities of a museum, many scholars have tended to ignore them. The black community, however, recognizes how King streets incorporate the Movement into the very language of the city and its inhabitants. Addresses are essential to daily activities and represent an important way of inscribing commemorative meanings into a multitude of urban practices and narratives. For many African Americans, the naming of streets for King is a search to find the most appropriate place to carry on his work. In conducting this search, the legitimacy and resonance of Dr. King's legacy is evaluated in relation to the character and reputation of the renamed street.

Just as proponents of street naming are sensitive to where King is commemorated, opponents are also concerned about the locational implications of commemoration. The same can be said of civil rights memorials more generally: activists are often unsuccessful in their efforts to commemorate the Movement outside the black community. Both street-renaming campaigns and civil rights museums have struggled against opposition based on financial concerns, racial bias, and a reluctance to delve into an emotion-laden past. Where a memorial is located and how it came to be there says a lot about "where" the nation is politically with regard to civil rights. It is telling that memorials to the Civil Rights Movement are the result of concerted efforts: they do not arise out of thin air to commemorate the worthy from our collective past; rather, they are sites *at* and *through* which activists attempt to link the past, present, and future into a coherent whole. They are potent symbolic resources, used to influence the future by shaping the past in accord with the needs of the present. As such, memorials are politically charged places. Despite the appearance of consensus and stability that characterizes memorials, they are both the product of, and conduit for, ongoing political debate.

The questions "Where?" and "How?" disclose the multiple interests at play in the creation of civil rights memorials. As we consider the broader implications of this geography of memory, the operative question becomes, "Why are they located here and *not* there?"

Chapter Three
Civil Rights Memorials: An Uneven Geography

Making sense of the interconnected strands of politics and economics that shape civil rights memorials benefits from an investigation of their location on the cultural landscape. More than an inert backdrop, the cultural landscape influences a memorial's meaning insofar as it simultaneously draws meaning from and gives meaning to its surroundings. Further, the social significance of a civil rights memorial cannot be fully appreciated beyond its geographic context. As discussed previously, civil rights memorials are not located in the places where Americans traditionally gather to commemorate the past; for instance, there are few civil rights memorials at courthouse lawns or along Main Street. Why are civil rights memorials located in some places but not others?

In this chapter, we examine the relative location of civil rights memorials at three different scales: regional, urban, and the neighborhood. The location of these sites in the South, in major cities, and in black neighborhoods is a telling indicator of the "place" occupied by the Movement's legacy in society. More generally, close inspection of the regional and urban geography of civil rights memorials suggests "where" the nation is presently "located" with regard to social justice. Regionally, civil rights memorials are clustered in the South—a fact consonant with the predominant, Won-Cause understanding of the Movement. Taking this regional pattern for granted, however, obscures a fuller understanding of the Movement and its legacy. Specifically, why are Movement-era campaigns in the North and on the West Coast not commemorated on the cultural landscape? At the metropolitan scale, the lack of civil rights memorials in traditional places of commemoration calls attention to the racialized condition of collective memory. Further, arguments over the most appropriate place for collective memory highlight the conflicts that ensue when antagonistic histories are commemorated in close proximity. The location of civil rights memorials straddles the border between remembering and forgetting, insofar as it raises an uncomfortable question: Do memorials *celebrate* these places or are they *confined* to them?

Memorial Entrepreneurs and the Regional Geography of Commemoration

In the predawn hours of December 4, 1969, the Chicago Police, in conjunction with the Federal Bureau of Investigation (FBI), stormed a Black Panther Party's safe house. In the process, they killed party members Mark Clark and Fred Hampton and wounded four others. The assault was part of the FBI's murderously successful Counter Intelligence Program (COINTELPRO). Among other actions, the program targeted Movement activists and organizations via a network of misinformation, paid informants, agent provocateurs, and assassinations. Subsequent trial proceedings contradicted the official story of a Black Panther ambush and disclosed a coordinated police attack followed by an attempted cover-up. COINTELPRO targeted a host of other civil rights-era organizations in addition to the Black Panthers, including Martin Luther King, Jr.'s SCLC and the Student Nonviolent Coordinating Committee (SNCC). In the eyes of the nation's power brokers, these groups—despite their different means and methods—appeared united in a vast conspiracy. When geographer Kenneth Foote conducted his seminal study of the places of violence and tragedy, he noted that the scene of Clark and Hampton's killing was still a private residence.[1] More recently, the house was razed to make way for gentrification in the area.[2] The condition of the site stands in mute contrast to the multi-million dollar shrines erected at the site of King's murder in Memphis, his final resting place in Atlanta, and his most famous campaign in Birmingham.

This commemorative unevenness is evident in street naming as well. While hundreds of roads have been identified with Martin Luther King, Jr., other activists, such as Hampton and Clark, are not household names for most Americans. Recent events in Chicago demonstrate the politics that come with remembering the Movement's more radical histories and historical figures. When Alderman Madeline Haithcock sponsored an ordinance that would attach Fred Hampton's name to a small, one-block section of West Monroe Street near where the Black Panther leader died, the proposal sparked vehement protests from members of the city's Fraternal Order of Police. They argued that Hampton incited violence against police by using phrases such as "off the pigs."[3] Supporters of Hampton defended his legacy and reputation by reminding the public of the brutal way in which law enforcement treated the black community in the 1960s, as well as some of the

Panther's less militant activities, such as organizing medical clinics, breakfast programs for children, and food and clothing depositories.[4] In March 2006, in a scene reminiscent of the King Street naming protests in Chattanooga, members of the Illinois Black Panther Party marched to the 2300 block of Monroe and posted their own homemade street signs with Hampton's name, although this protest did not have the same successful outcome as the one in Chattanooga.[5] The different treatment of these sites—some remembered, others forgotten—reflects in microcosm the uneven treatment the Movement receives on the cultural landscape.

Gaps and inconsistencies in how the Movement is commemorated are derived in part from the coalitions that produce memorials. As discussed in our introduction, "memorial entrepreneurs" do not necessarily profit financially from the past; rather, the memorial entrepreneur is any enterprising individual who influences the presentation of collective memory. In this model, commemoration is a custodial process in which individuals shape how the public conceives of and interprets the past. Successful memorial entrepreneurs are marked by a number of qualities, ranging from the intensity of their motivation to the extent of their political connections. For instance, it is unlikely that any public monument can overcome the inevitable objections and opposition without a full measure of devotion and dedication on the part of its proponents. Further, commemoration obliges its proponents to present a plausible account of the past. Wishful thinking, cant, and outright fabrication are difficult to get through a committee. Of particular importance is the ability of entrepreneurs to work and build coalitions with others who have the same commemorative goals, though they may not share them for the same reasons. Public commemoration requires cooperation from a wide array of individuals, groups, and agencies. Given this interconnectedness and the high stakes, it is not surprising that the process can be contentious. Thus, the entrepreneur's degree of interest in the task, his/her narrative facility or clarity, and his/her position vis-à-vis networks of power all influence the production of a memorial.[6]

The work of Fath Davis Ruffins suggests that the roots of civil rights memorial entrepreneurism lie in the late 1960s, when many civil rights activists began pursuing their agenda through the creation of cultural institutions.[7] Until this time, black cultural institutions were limited to churches and segregated colleges. Faced with legislative defeats and white backlash, activists identified cultural politics as an alternative way to promote social change. Many activists sought to exert control over the production of knowledge for and about African-American experiences. One result of this desire was the creation of more than 100 African-American museums since 1950. Created alongside these museums were a large number of art galleries, performing arts academies, festivals, conferences, and academic departments. In a host of media, ranging from books to paintings and dance to theater, cultural activists challenged the popular conflation of public history with the history of white men and set the Movement in a broader historical context of Africa, slavery, and international anticolonial struggles. A defining feature of these new institutions was their efforts to develop talent and political consciousness rather than act as a vanguard by setting standards of style and criticism. In contrast to elite black institutions that reached relatively few people, these new institutions emphasized serving a broad audience. With initially small collections and staffs, they worked to foster strong networks of supporters, visitors, and volunteers—networks that have been crucial to developing collections, programming, and continuing operations in an era of decreased federal funding for the arts.

It was in this context that Frances Smiley of Alabama's Bureau of Tourism and Travel began promoting black heritage tourism.[8] The first African-American professional at the bureau, Smiley was initially assigned the task of promoting group tourism. With the support of her immediate supervisor, she organized a marketing campaign to spread the message that the state had changed in the wake of desegregation. The intended effect of this message was to entice the state's many African-American emigrants to consider returning for a vacation or longer. Importantly, she promoted a nuanced rendering of the African-American past, one that did more than simply highlight the birthplaces of athletes and entertainers.

As a result of Smiley's efforts, Alabama produced the nation's first statewide guide to African-American history, *Alabama's Black Heritage*. In magazine format, the guide presented maps, glossy color photos, and tour routes associated with black history. Its publication in 1983 caught the attention of newspapers across the country. Alabama's governor at the time was George Wallace, and the national media savored the irony of the former arch-segregationist promoting African-American history. Contrary to detractors who predicted that no audience existed for such a guide, hundreds of copies of *Alabama's*

Black Heritage were requested during its first week in publication. After four months, the first print run of 18,500 copies was exhausted. Since then, the guide has gone through four editions, the number of sites listed has increased from fifty-four to 163, and 650,000 copies have been distributed worldwide. The majority of requests for the magazine come from travel professionals who recognize the great potential of the African-American heritage market.

Interviews with tourism officials and the widespread presence of state-sponsored literature promoting civil rights tourism testify to the desire on the part of elected officials to rectify simultaneously their public image and to attract tourist dollars. Increasingly, cities and states market their local history in pursuit of capital investment and consumer spending. Faced with reduced federal support, declining tax bases, and increasingly fluid national and international markets, cities and states recognize heritage tourism as a strategy for economic development. Cognizant of the positive publicity generated by promotional literature, such as *Alabama's Black Heritage*, states and private tour operators across the nation copied Alabama's efforts and produced heritage guides of their own. Philadelphia, Pennsylvania's multicultural tourism agency accounts for nearly half of the $200 million in tourist-generated revenue for the city in any given year. African-American spending on travel and tourism has grown significantly since 1980—a fact not lost on local boosters or the tourism industry. In light of the considerable amount of money involved in this sort of tourism—the Travel Industry Association of America estimates that a tour bus of twenty-eight to thirty-two people spends upwards of $5,000 to $7,000 per day on travel-related goods and services—it is not surprising that government and private tourism promoters actively support a heroic recounting of the Movement.

Thus, the rise of civil rights memorials across the South is the result of a complex mix of activism and commercial promotion. By turn complementary and contradictory, drawing clear distinctions between these commingled impulses is difficult. Producing a memorial typically involves cobbling together a powerful, albeit temporary, coalition of groups with diverse interests. In the case of civil rights memorials, this coalition often brings together activists with representatives of the Chamber of Commerce—two groups that, under different circumstances, often clash. Both parties, however, recognize that it is in their best interest to promote commemoration of the Movement. Thus, civil rights memorials cannot be understood as purely the result of activism or commercialism but rather as an ambiguous blend of both, one that often involves conflicting sympathies, temporary alliances, and occasional co-option. In the South, diverse parties have tended to coalesce around an understanding of the Movement as something that has already occurred. This coalescence is hampered—in the South and beyond—when the conversation about the Movement broadens to include an unfinished, contemporary agenda of de facto racial discrimination.

While a particular version of the Movement has been commemorated as a result of these efforts, critics charge that the costs and benefits of such tourism are not well balanced, calling attention to the limited employment opportunities created by museums, exacerbated traffic congestion, and harmful side effects of gentrification on surrounding areas. For instance, while civil rights memorials attract large tour groups, very few of these visitors eat at the restaurants located in the immediate vicinity. Typically, the restaurants are either situated in visually inconspicuous or blighted areas or they are too small to service tour groups. Instead, the tourists climb back on the bus and eat at the commercial chains usually located outside the black part of town, a condition that speaks to the ongoing de facto segregation in these cities. Critics also charge that, in some instances, white consulting firms with insider connections have won memorial-related contracts while African Americans with more civil rights experience but less lucrative connections have been overlooked.

Further complicating the role of tourism bureaus are the guides they produce. For a mass audience largely unfamiliar with the intricacies of the Movement's history, these guides play the role of gatekeeper, selecting which sites are appropriate for the general public. For instance, Robert Weyeneth reports that Illinois's Tourism Bureau removed any reference to the site of the deaths of Black Panthers Clark and Hampton from its guide. Subsequently, the Pepperbird Foundation, a nonprofit organization that promotes African-American history, included the site of the shooting in its guide to Chicago. In the case of *Alabama's Black Heritage*, the magazine makes only passing reference to Lowndes County. Located between Selma and Montgomery, Lowndes was a hotbed of SNCC organizing. Working with local activists, SNCC's field officer, Stokely Carmichael, organized the original Black Panther Party and ran an independent slate of candidates for public office. Their efforts laid the groundwork for the Voting Rights March and resulted in the first African Americans elected to county office since Reconstruction. Nevertheless, SNCC and Carmichael are not mentioned in *Alabama's Black Heritage*.

The lack of attention garnered by the Black Panthers and SNCC's efforts in Lowndes County suggests the extent to which the Won Cause interpretation of the Movement shapes the geography of civil rights memorials, suggesting an inaccurate picture of where the Movement happened and where it did not. For memorial entrepreneurs seeking to solidify (often quite literally in granite and marble) the legitimacy of their office, to attract capital, and to promote consumption, the Won Cause offers a way to distinguish themselves from the past and to project a progressive image into the future. On the contrary, Clark and Hampton's apartment and Lowndes County do not perform the same function. These stories raise the specter of state-sponsored assassinations and black militancy—topics that remain outside the Won Cause's celebration of integration and nonviolent protest. A similar fate befalls Movement-era campaigns that do not conform to the strictures of the Won Cause: fair housing in Chicago, school reform in New York City, and police brutality in Los Angeles. Because most memorial entrepreneurs cannot envision a tour of lost or unresolved civil rights campaigns, civil rights memorials cluster in the South around a few successful campaigns for voting rights and against *de jure* segregation. And while it rightly celebrates stories of sacrifice and heroism, the Won Cause diminishes our collective memory of the Movement's radical potential.

Emphasis on the Won Cause version of the Movement—as opposed to a more complex and ambiguous retelling of this tumultuous period—is in keeping with the selective appropriation of local history for economic development and public relations. This was certainly the case in Memphis, where city leaders backed the development of the National Civil Rights Museum for the explicit purpose of dealing with the city's role as the site of King's assassination. Their intention was to create a memorial that acknowledged the event and shifted attention to the Movement's success. The same desire to put the past in its place occurred in Birmingham and was instrumental in the development of the city's museum. As former Birmingham mayor and Civil Rights Institute supporter David Vann commented, "I've always said the best way to put your bad images to rest is to declare them history and put them in a museum."[9] The desire to rectify the city's image—it was popularly known as "Bombingham"—along with increased tourist revenues consolidated the support of the local corporate community behind the project. Most civil rights memorials, with their emphasis on accomplishment and transcendence, confirm this desire to leave the past behind. For David Vann and others, civil rights memorials put history in what they consider to be a safe, neutral place: a museum.

The separation of past and present is, however, not hard and fast. For many activists, the production of civil rights memorials, whatever their limitations, is better than nothing at all, inasmuch as forging a strong link between the past and future can be the beginning of a thorough critique of contemporary racism. In contrast to those who want to place boundaries around the Movement, there are activists such as those at the National Voting Rights Museum in Selma. The museum's volunteer staff works diligently to overcome the partition between the past and present by representing time and place in less static terms. Visitors can read biographical sketches of local organizers, past and present. The museum's docent, Joanne Bland, takes visitors on a tour of Selma that mixes historical and contemporary aspects of the Movement. Paramount among the concerns of the museum's staff is the desire to connect in the minds of young people the heroism of local Movement personalities with the contemporary struggle against racism. For these memorial entrepreneurs, the cultural landscape can reinforce their claim that the Movement remains unfinished business.

Both David Vann, of Birmingham, and Joanne Bland, of Selma, undoubtedly support the creation of civil rights museums and their promotion by the tourism industry. Nevertheless, neither one can afford to ignore the essentially unsettled meaning of memorials. All parties concerned with collective memory must be prepared to contend with the multiple, sometimes contradictory interpretations of the Movement that memorials inspire among visitors. By linking a place with the Movement, a memorial can be interpreted as an endorsement or an indictment, an aid to remembering or to forgetting.

Memory Space in the City

The majority of sites related to campaigns outside the South remain formally un-marked because their stories invite unfavorable comparison with contemporary conditions for African Americans and other people of color, including de facto segregation, oppressive police, the absence of local school control, and redlining. And while these themes cannot be incorporated into tourism's focus on the triumphant or transcendent, civil rights memorials still tend to be located amid the declining remains of segregation-era black business districts and neighborhoods. These areas are characterized by the racialized aftershocks of suburbanization and urban renewal programs: neighborhoods and businesses replaced by vacant lots and parking garages; overhead highway interchanges; low-end retail establishments and falling real estate values; abandoned warehouses and derelict industrial infrastructure. The neighborhoods near most civil rights memorials are predominantly African-American, and their conditions—dilapidated housing stock, high unemployment, poor transportation, declining schools, and violent drug trade—speak to the limitations of the very changes wrought by the events of the 1950s and 60s. These conditions belie the triumphal, Won Cause rhetoric of the memorials they host.

Nevertheless, the site of these memorials is neither surprising nor inappropriate. Their location among black-owned businesses and churches affirms the central role played by these institutions in the Movement; these are the sites at which history literally took place. Mass meetings, a centerpiece of the Movement, were held in African-American churches. Black-owned businesses were an important source of leadership and financial support. The presence of local churches and businesses pays heed to their long history of resisting racism, practices that informed the Movement and provided the context out of which it grew.

The placement of civil rights memorials in historically African-American areas marks a point of convergence between the black community's history and the contemporary promotion of heritage tourism. Current trends in American public history emphasize site-specific representations in order to promote an authentic experience of the past. These efforts to promote site-based public history intersect with the efforts of activists to use preservation as a tactic for consolidating and extending the Movement's achievements. Activists in Memphis resisted the suggestion that the Lorraine Motel be torn down as a blemish on the city's reputation and that King be remembered with a statue elsewhere in the city. While King's legacy is commemorated with a downtown installation, activists placed great importance on preserving the actual site of King's murder—in no small part because the visceral quality of place helps to create a sense of a tangible and immediate past. For memorial entrepreneurs who want simultaneously to define the Movement's legacy and to organize a constituency for the future, historic preservation is crucial.

Placing civil rights memorials amid the remains of historically black neighborhoods and business districts thus highlights a rich historical context. In a similar manner, their *non-location* relative to the traditional places of civic memory—City Hall, the courthouse lawn, and Main Street—calls attention to the racial politics of collective memory. Their absence at these places is a reminder that the majority of public history sites are uniformly white. The rise of civil rights memorials at sites removed from the courthouse lawn and Main Street subtly de-centers civic memory and enriches the cultural landscape. Placing civil rights memorials away from the town center, with its government buildings and war memorials, and toward the remnants of the African- American business district recognizes new public spaces. For instance, in both Birmingham and Memphis, specific proposals for creating memorials were couched in terms of coming to terms with the past in order to create a more democratic city.

Nevertheless, the lack of recognition of civil rights history at City Hall and along Main Street raises a concern: in addition to celebrating the Movement's heritage sites, these memorials may be confined to them—confined, in the sense that, if organizers had so desired, could they have secured a site for these memorials outside of predominantly African-American neighborhoods and placed them within the traditional core of civic memory? Research into the politics of naming streets in honor of Martin Luther King, Jr. suggests it is unlikely. Across the nation, street-naming opponents consistently impose strict spatial limits on such proposals, in effect seeking to constrain proposed memorials to black areas of cities. As one Atlanta journalist pointed out in evaluating named streets as symbols of unity and equality, "[King's name] is on streets everywhere. . . . everywhere except the white part of town. . . . The geographical reality of King's asphalt legacy is more about boundaries than about bridges."[10] The sad irony is that, while Dr. King challenged segregation, his memory is often fixed at a scale that reinforces contemporary racial divisions and inequalities.

In conventional geographic terms, "scale" refers to the relative extent of an object in space; colloquially, it expresses the perceived extent of a problem, commonly ranging from the local to the global. Fixing the extent of an issue's spatial relevance is a value-laden choice; that is, scale becomes political when there is a meaningful difference between describing an event as "merely local" or of "international importance." The history of the bus boycott in Montgomery and the subsequent struggle over its memorial legacy offers a case in point of what geographer Neil Smith calls the "double-edged nature" of scale to constrain or enlarge the visibility of a cause or social identity.[11] With the significant exception of the African-American press, newspapers within and outside the South routinely ignored or gave marginal attention to the struggle of blacks for equal public accommodations. Bus and trolley boycotts had been staged across the region long before they occurred in Montgomery. Invariably, they were labeled as "local" disturbances related to the "peculiar" condition of race relations in the South, the implication being that, in the wake of failed Reconstruction-era policies, the rest of the country should mind its own business and let Southern whites have their way.

One reason the Montgomery bus boycott successfully attracted broad attention was its organizers' acumen in rescaling the conflict from a local issue of municipal transport into a matter of human rights in the context of a global Cold War. In Martin Luther King, Jr., local activists found a spokesman who could articulate the contradiction between oppression at home and America's struggle to win hearts and minds abroad in Africa, Asia, and South America. In light of the nation's successful war against fascism in Europe and the Pacific, and its confrontation with the totalitarian Soviet bloc, the usual dismissal of the bus boycott as part of the South's so-called "Negro problem" failed to address the negative reflection the incident conveyed to an international audience. In effect, the Movement, with King as its spokesman, advantageously rescaled the struggle against segregation.

Despite the important role that the bus boycott played in dismantling legalized segregation, memorial entrepreneurs in Montgomery have confronted significant obstacles when attempting to memorialize the Movement beyond the confines of the African-American community. This resistance became apparent in Montgomery in 1972, when the city commission rescinded a decision to name a street for King after the local White Citizens Coalition (WCC) objected. According to Roger Stump, the WCC was angered because the renamed street contained white-owned businesses and a white Masonic lodge. A leader of the WCC stated that he had no problem with honoring King so long as the street was located entirely within the black part of the city.[12]

Seventeen years later, African Americans in Keysville, Georgia, a smaller rural community, met little resistance when they renamed a street for King within the limits of the city where blacks comprise more than three-quarters of the population. Black leaders, however, encountered intense opposition when they sought to have the road renamed through the entire county, which is almost fifty percent white. Ultimately, county commissioners voted against the geographic extension of Martin Luther King Road. Keysville's mayor, Emma Greshman, reacted to the decision, saying, "The whites who protested the new name need a little more knowledge about what Dr. King meant not only to his race but to America."[13] For Gresham, the scale at which King is commemorated is important because it can heighten or diminish the impact of his memory on traditional, white-centered interpretations of the past. And while the place of Keysville's King Road on the margins of collective memory can substantiate calls for justice, it comes at the price of a location that can be ignored as being narrowly "racial."

Unlike civil rights museums, which enjoy the support of tourism-related businesses, the business community seldom welcomes street-renaming proposals, thus playing an influential role in restricting the scale at which the Movement is commemorated. Women activists in Gainesville, Georgia, finally persuaded their city council to rename Myrtle Street, an east-west connector road, for King in 2000. After three unsuccessful bids, the group adjusted its original proposal—under pressure from business and property owners along the street—and suggested renaming a small portion of the road.[14] Afterward, the leader of the street-naming effort, Faye Bush, remarked that, while winning the name struggle energized black leaders, it also opened their eyes to "how hard it is to get even little things changed."[15] In 1987, city officials in St. Petersburg, Florida, reached a compromise with business interests over the renaming issue: the street retained two official names, and property owners could choose either to identify with King Street or to retain their Ninth Street address.[16] A strict geographic scaling of King's commemoration by race resulted: whites at the north end of the street used Ninth Street on business cards and phonebook listings while African-American neighborhoods on the southern end aligned themselves with the civil rights leader.[17] The dual naming existed for fifteen years until local NAACP and SCLC leaders requested that the city drop Ninth Street signs.[18] While some businesses on Ninth Street/Martin Luther King, Jr. street complained, the opposition was not nearly as large as in 1987, reflecting not only the liberalization of attitudes, but also, and perhaps more importantly, the street's changing racial/ethnic composition. As a reporter observed at the time, "More black families—and Hispanic and Asian and eastern European ones—have moved into the neighborhoods along the northern section of the street, replacing many of the white retirees who used to dominate the area."[19]

When confronted with proposals to rename a street for King, business owners typically complain about the financial burden of changing their address on mailing labels, advertising, and stationery. This argument would appear to be simply a matter of cost and convenience, but it sometimes hides a deeper protection of racial boundaries. This was the case in 2003, when African-American leaders in Quincy, Illinois, compromised their proposal and agreed to have Eighth Street designated in honor of King rather than legally renaming the street. Privately funded honorary signs were to be placed along Eighth Street; however, when activists sought to have King signs attached to every sign pole along the street, including the largely white southern end, the proposal encountered significant opposition. Despite the fact that no addresses would be changed and private contributions funded the signs, only select intersections were marked.[20] In explaining their opposition, some whites on South Eighth feared that the increased visibility of King's name would detract from their attempts to promote the city's German heritage, and they argued for concentrating the signs in the more African-American, northern portion of the street.[21]

Although most business owners couch their opposition to street-naming proposals as economic and not racially motivated, it is often difficult to separate these claims from the emotional memories of past racial tensions. For instance, in Muncie, Indiana, Ed McCloud responded to the changing of his address from Broadway to Martin Luther King by closing his appliance business of fifty years. While McCloud expressed concern that a new address might have confused customers and prevented them from finding his store, he also remembered an incident vividly when one of his earlier stores had been set on fire by rioters following King's assassination in 1968. McCloud added: "I swore then that I would not let the black community—or anyone else—hurt my business again."[22]

Ed McCloud perhaps represents an exaggerated response to the street-naming process. Indeed, in 2004, one year after the city council of Eugene, Oregon, renamed Centennial

Boulevard for King, business representatives on the street reported that the economic impact of the address change was negligible.[23] Nevertheless, many opponents voice concern that their businesses will suffer from being identified with the African-American community. Recall the earlier discussion of Chattanooga, Tennessee, where a prominent real estate developer argued that he could not rent office space along King Street because of its racial overtones. Similar objections were raised in Safety Harbor, Florida, in 1990, when an African-American civic group proposed renaming Fourth Street, an important commercial street connecting several neighborhoods. In opposing the proposal, the city manager expressed concern that the renaming would lower property values along the street.[24] Although appraisers went on record that renaming a street has no effect on property values, the opposition circulated a petition that made the (eventually successful) renaming process even more contentious.[25]

Concerns about the impact of street naming on property values and business profits is part of a much larger anxiety on the part of whites about living and working on King streets. African-American comedian Chris Rock famously declared in his HBO comedy series, "If a friend calls you on the telephone and says they're lost on Martin Luther King Boulevard and they want to know what they should do, the best response is, 'Run.'"[26] Rock's satire is meant to prompt his audience to question and change the status quo, but, ironically, his words have been used by street-naming opponents to fuel assertions that a King address is a social stigma. Jonathan Tilove perhaps puts it best when he writes, "It has become a commonplace of popular culture to identify a Martin Luther King street as a generic marker of black space and not incidentally, of ruin, as a sad signpost of danger, failure, and decline. . . ."[27] To illustrate his point, Tilove describes a situation in which a white homeowner in Boynton Beach, Florida, sought to have King's name removed from a nearby road, fearing that a potential buyer of his townhouse would avoid purchasing near such an address. Speaking with a local newspaper reporter, the homeowner explained what streets he thought should be identified with King: "I didn't buy across the railroad tracks. All of a sudden the railroad tracks is over here. So I don't live in the ghetto. Why is the name there?"[28]

There is no evidence to suggest that street naming is necessarily bad for business. Although resistance from business interests has significantly limited the scale of King's commemoration, large numbers of commercial establishments can be found on several streets named for the civil rights leader (for example, in Tampa, Florida; Atlanta, Georgia; Lansing, Michigan; Los Angeles, California; Houston, Texas; and New Bern, North Carolina). Analyzing the almost 11,000 non-residential establishments in the nation with a Martin Luther King address, Matthew Mitchelson found these establishments to be on par with national trends in terms of annual sales volume and number of employees. He also found, however, that King streets are "less industrially diverse than other places" and "host a disproportionately high number of establishments traditionally categorized as 'black businesses,' such as beauty parlors and barber shops, small retail grocery stores, and funeral parlors."[29]

King's memory does not necessarily cause poverty and degradation along streets; rather, his name is often placed in poorer areas as a result of public opposition to naming more prominent places. In Portland, Oregon, for example, Union Avenue had been in decline long before being renamed for King. Some people within the Portland Development Commission suggest that the decline began as early as 1924 with "an overly permissive commercial code that resulted in lowering of property values and poor quality construction."[30] By the time that members of the city council renamed Union Avenue for King in 1989, the street's black community had already seen significant losses in jobs, housing, and businesses as well as the emergence of drug-related gang activity.[31] For more than fifteen years, Portland's King Boulevard has undergone urban renewal. This has led to a 300 percent increase in the street's residential values between 1993 and 2003, although some areas of King Boulevard are still in need of revitalization.[32]

Perhaps the most glaring example of the influence wielded by business interests in the street-naming process comes from Statesboro, Georgia. In their second attempt to attach King's name to a major thoroughfare, African Americans targeted Northside Drive, the location of more than 250 businesses. As a result of business opposition, city officials passed an ordinance that required name-change proposals to obtain the approval of seventy-five percent of property owners along the street in question and to pay half the cost of changing street signs.[33] After the passage of the ordinance, a Statesboro city councilman spent approximately six months going door to door to collect signatures from property owners along a smaller, poorer, and largely African-American street. While many people thought a named street was long overdue, some opponents questioned whether the chosen street was prominent enough to honor King.[34]

Other cities and towns in the United States have established similar ordinances. For example, in Zephyrhills, Florida, which drew national attention when it named a street for King and then rescinded in 2004, members of City Council responded to the controversy by passing an ordinance that not only calls for seventy-five percent of property owners to support a name change, but also specifies that numerical and alphabetical street names can not be changed.[35] This seriously limits the possibility of renaming many downtown streets and again diminishes the scale at which King is commemorated. Such ordinances make street renaming difficult since it is unlikely that commercial stakeholders along a major street would support the proposal. Moreover, longer and more prominent streets typically have many street signs. This significantly increases the funds needed to honor King whose name usually requires a longer and more expensive sign. Running through these ordinances is a reactionary understanding of community in which the interests of property and business owners are valued over those other stakeholders, such as those who rent, work, or simply drive down the street. The ordinances allow cities to enact a vision of public space not open and receptive to all city citizens but territorialized, privatized, and controlled.

As a consequence of these ordinances, and opposition in general, some activists have washed their hands of Main Street altogether and instead have attempted to use King's name as a springboard for economic development within the African-American community. In fact, several King-named streets in the country are the focus of significant revitalization efforts, such as those in Jersey City, New Jersey, Savannah, Georgia, Seattle, Washington, and Miami, Florida. Miami's multicultural initiative for cleaning up and renovating its Dr. Martin Luther King, Jr. Boulevard is called "Reclaim the Dream." In Elizabeth City, North Carolina, the director of the city's neighborhood community development corporation campaigned to have Martin Street, named after an early physician, changed to Martin Luther King Street. She attempted to connect King's legacy with ongoing attempts to revitalize African-American business and residential areas. In her words:

"[t]he street is just the kind of street where King did much of his work. . . . Being small and having traffic lights and stop signs doesn't make it less worthy to be named Martin Luther King Drive. . . . Martin Luther King didn't work along the freeway. He worked in communities."[36]

These efforts resonate with those who want to preserve the Movement's racial identity. Some activists fear that commemorating the Movement outside of black communities inevitably leads to compromises intended to appeal to a broader audience out of touch with contemporary African-American concerns. With this in mind, one of the major issues confronting plans to redevelop King's namesakes is that poor, black populations will be further marginalized. In developing its King Street, the city of Allentown, Pennsylvania, evicted the residents of "Tent City," a group of makeshift dwellings occupied by homeless people.[37] The revitalization of the western portion of Greenville, North Carolina, drew formal protests from black leaders who feared that city leaders planned to rid black, low-order businesses from Martin Luther King, Jr. Drive and to displace minority renters for white homeowners.[38]

Struggles to commemorate King are both intra- and inter-racial. Robert S., a black radio show host in Grand Rapids, Michigan, successfully challenged the established African-American leadership when the city accepted his idea of designating or dedicating a street for King rather than formally renaming one.[39] Robert's proposal gained widespread support among his young, inner-city black listeners who helped him raise more than $27,000 to pay for commemorative signs for the street.[40] Although the dedicated street is a major north-south artery in the city and, ironically, is named Division Avenue, some black opponents argued that the honorary designation did not convey the same dignity as an official change of address.[41] Tensions within the black community also surfaced in San Jose, California, when a retired police officer made the seemingly convenient proposal to have King Street, named after nineteenth-century farmer Andrew King, reidentified for the civil rights leader. Latinos adamantly opposed the renaming of King Street, which runs through San Jose's largest Mexican-American neighborhood and was the site of marches led by labor leader Cesar Chavez. Wishing to avoid racial/ethnic conflict, leaders of the local NAACP wrote a letter to city officials supporting the Latino opposition and the eventual abandonment of the road-naming request.[42]

Embracing different political goals, African-American leaders sometimes disagree with each other over which street to name in honor of Martin Luther King, Jr. Even in Chattanooga, where black leaders formed an impressive coalition, a particularly outspoken activist wished to see King's name on a street in a "better part of town," contending that much of Ninth Street was characterized by crime and marginal economic activity. NAACP leader George Key countered by asserting that a renamed Ninth Street "would be a symbol to let young blacks know that there is something in Chattanooga they can identify with. . . . to have the feeling that Chattanooga cares about its black people."[43] Eatonton, Georgia, had a more visible competition between two African-American leaders—one lobbied for the renaming of a major highway that ran through the length of town while the other convinced local officials to rename a residential street within the black community. While the memorial entrepreneur who advocated for the thoroughfare emphasized the use of Dr. King's memory to challenge and expand the historical consciousness of whites, the other activist emphasized how the renaming of the residential street would focus and inspire African Americans.[44] For this activist, King's memory should be scaled to fit the black community more closely, lest it be the subject of seemingly endless debates or co-opted like so many African-American innovations. For some memorial entrepreneurs, King's memory rightly belongs in the black part of town.

I Wish I Was in Dixie and You Weren't

Is African-American history being shut out of America's traditional places of memory or is the nation's cultural landscape being broadened to include a wider diversity of places? Certainly, the inclusion of new historical venues in the canon of public history is in line with the goals of the Movement to open society to African Americans. But could it also be the case that segregationists have simply conceded the point that African Americans have a history worth remembering all the while seeking to keep American history divided into racial boxes? Has the arrival of memorials in the 'hood signaled a new kind of ghetto, one that bottles up and contains African-American history? Or does recognizing the dignity of these places take us one step closer to the establishment of King's "Beloved

Community"? These questions—which revolve around issues of perception and intent—cannot be answered definitively. Recent events in Selma, Alabama, however, offer a pithy lesson in the complexities of commemorating antagonistic histories in the same place. The partially successful attempt of a neo-Confederate group to commemorate the failed defense of Selma during the Civil War demonstrates the manner in which civil rights and Civil War commemoration display an uncomfortable symmetry, with advances in one seemingly prompting advances in the other. Further, the affair offers a cautionary tale for anyone ready to declare the matter of race a moot point on the memorial landscape.

While traditionally the domain of white elites, Confederate commemoration has undergone a radical reworking over the past fifty years. Since the 1950s, working-class whites opposed to integration have claimed the memory of the Confederacy, especially its battle flag—a blue St. Andrew's cross with thirteen stars set against a red field, the so-called Stars and Bars—as a bulwark against racial integration. Among the groups active on this front has been the League of the South, a nationalist organization with the avowed goal of reconstituting the Southern Confederacy. The League promotes a theological interpretation of the Civil War, casting the Confederacy and its supporters as Christian warriors who fought valiantly against the secular, capitalist North—a position that is gaining in popularity among neo-Confederate groups.[45]

The shift in the Confederacy's memorial constituency and its new sense of purpose is symbolized by the rising popularity of the Confederate cavalry officer—and failed defender of Selma—Nathan Bedford Forrest. A two-fisted slave trader and land speculator, Forrest rose from the rank of private to general during the course of the war. Known to supporters as the "Wizard of the Saddle" and described by an adversary as the "Devil himself," Forrest's reputation has grown at the expense of the man who most embodied patrician sensibilities, Robert E. Lee. Neo-Confederates see in Forrest the sort of rugged, self-made man with whom latter-day, working-class Confederates can identify. The shift, registered in terms of new memorials, biographies, and, most ubiquitously, commemorative bumper stickers and t-shirts, has been lamented by the older, more established proponents of Confederate memory as a vulgar corruption of their cause. As a result, commemoration of the Confederacy, formerly an elite undertaking, now has a decidedly proletarian and overtly racialized edge to it.

The recent controversy in Selma hinged on a dispute over the proper place for a bronze bust of Forrest. Unveiled in October 2000, the bust sits atop a five-ton granite base inscribed with milestones from his military career and sundry Confederate insignia, among them a color reproduction of the Stars and Bars. Erected by a group calling themselves the "Friends of Forrest," of which some were active in the League of the South, the monument was placed on the grounds of a city-owned, antebellum house/museum—in the midst of a predominantly African-American neighborhood. Funds for the monument were privately raised, notably with little involvement from the older, more established Confederate memorial groups, such as the United Daughters of the Confederacy. The dedication ceremony included prayers and speeches by members of the League of the South and other neo-Confederate groups. The tenor of the meeting was suggested by the comment of a city policeman assigned to the event's security detail who described it for the local paper as "a Klan meeting without the hoods."[46]

Significantly, the monument was erected only a week after Selma's first black mayor, James Perkins, Jr., bested the city's previous mayor of thirty-six years, Joe Smitherman. Like his political mentor George Wallace, the late governor of Alabama, Smitherman was a political survivor. Coming into office a few months before the Voting Rights March in 1965, Smitherman opposed the Movement. In the wake of its victory, however, he adjusted with the times and managed to stay in office in a black-majority city. The stark contrast between Smitherman's defeat—attributed to his advanced age and the militant opposition of local civil rights organizers to an unprecedented tenth term—and the Forrest commemoration attracted national attention. The media presented the twinned events—Smitherman's defeat and the subsequent emplacement of the Forrest monument in the midst of an African-American neighborhood—as evidence that the more things changed in Selma, the more they stayed the same. A local resident, quoted in the *Los Angeles Times*, echoed the media's portrayal of the situation: "You lose control of your city government and a week later you put up a statue to a Confederate general? How Southern. These heritage guys are basically saying what a lot of people around here feel: The fight goes on. The war never really ends."[47]

Kenneth Foote's concept of "symbolic accretion"—in which memorial entrepreneurs append commemorative elements onto extant memorials—offers a timely lens for understanding the complex interplay of collective memory and place-making which characterizes the Forrest affair.[48] Symbolic accretion is a strategy for enhancing the reputation of a cause via proximity with an established memorial landscape. For instance, consider that memorial entrepreneurs commonly seek out space on courthouse lawns. In doing so, they hope to legitimize their cause via close association with government's local seat. Their expectation is that affixing a memorial token will galvanize their cause with some measure of the hallowed qualities associated with its location, regardless of whether the site has little or no historical connection to the issue at hand. To wit, there is a plethora of Martin Luther King, Jr. streets in cities where he never set foot. The point of renaming such a street is not to commemorate an actual event but rather to burnish King's legacy in the glow of a valued public space. In so doing, memorial entrepreneurs rejuvenate and reinvest meaning in what would otherwise be a patch of grass or busy thoroughfare. The result is something akin to a symbiotic relationship between memorial places, such as courthouses, and nascent collective memories.

In the case of Selma, residents of the neighborhood and the city's civil rights community rallied against the attempt to place the Forrest monument outside the bounds of Selma's existing Confederate memorial. In addition to objecting to the placement of the monument on public property in the middle of their neighborhood, opponents criticized the omission of any reference to Forrest's pre-war career as a slave trader, his command role during the war-time massacre of black Union troops, and his post-war association with the Ku Klux Klan (KKK). Opponents were divided, however, as to how to remedy the situation. Some argued for a plaque or mural à la the new Liberty Monument in New Orleans that would disclose Forrest's role in oppressing African Americans—a rather canny expression of symbolic accretion whereby the intent was not to enhance but rather to detract from an established memorial. They sought to undermine the narrow interpretation of Forrest by bringing the monument into close proximity with a powerful counternarrative that explicitly raised the issue of racial oppression. Those in favor of this proposal believed that placing Forrest in a broader context would effectively undermine the celebratory interpretation of his career. Other opponents of the monument, however, were more concerned with its placement on public property in a black neighborhood. They favored the outright removal of the monument to the cemetery's Confederate memorial, thereby confining Confederate commemoration to a location already identified with the Lost Cause.

The Friends of Forrest countered by stressing that Smitherman had approved the monument's installation on public property two years earlier, albeit without any input from the majority black city council. Further, they argued that the racial composition of the surrounding neighborhood was irrelevant, in the process implying that raising the issue of race was divisive. They defended the monument's focus on Forrest's military career as a matter of choice and noted that he had voluntarily resigned from the KKK, albeit in anticipation of a federal law making membership illegal. This narrow focus on Forrest's military exploits corresponds to the general claim by neo-Confederates that their cause is one of "heritage, not hate." In keeping with this rhetorical position, Forrest was presented as a military hero who defended the Southland against invaders—a focus that sought to downplay his role in oppressing African Americans. Finally, they argued that the placement of the monument at a former field hospital and antebellum home was a more appropriate place for a war monument than a cemetery. Given the confrontational bearing of Forrest, aligning his monument with the genteel ambiance of the house/museum offered activists a way to deflect attention from less savory aspects of Forrest's career and the implicit challenge his monument posed to the African-American neighborhood.

Four months of long and contentious meetings of the city council ensued against a backdrop of protests, counterprotests, vandalism, and a failed attempt to topple the monument. A committee formed to study the issue recommended moving the monument inside the antebellum house museum and adding a plaque with a fuller accounting of Forrest's career. The recommendation satisfied neither party. Opponents of the monument, while eager to discuss Forrest's role in the KKK, continued to call for the outright removal of the monument to the cemetery. Supporters claimed that it was "intolerant" to insist that the monument be moved, and they fought any attempt to discuss Forrest's association with the KKK. In the wake of the polarizing debate, and under increasing pressure from Selma's business community to bring the fracas to an end, City Council rejected the proposal to amend the monument and voted to remove it, essentially accreting the Forrest monument onto the existing Confederate presence at the city cemetery. On the whole, the affair testifies to the shifting and uncertain condition of "collective memory":

a political process in which memorial entrepreneurs clash over the interpretation of past events, in effect, trying to condense and to harden and accrete one layer of meaning above all others.

Conclusion

Whether viewed across the nation as a whole or from the perspective of the struggle in a small city, such as Selma, commemoration is emphatically a political process of augmenting or disrupting the stories associated with a place. James Young, a historian who has written extensively about Holocaust memorials, described the relationship in terms of a primal struggle between remembering and forgetting.[49] After examining impressive Holocaust memorials throughout Israel, Europe, and the United States, he wondered if monuments may act to displace the responsibility of remembering from the living and actually serve the purpose of forgetting. By necessity, however, monuments do both. Commemoration involves some element of forgetting, inasmuch as a monument condenses memory, dislodging it from its context and focusing scarce attention on the particular at the expense of the whole, or vice versa. As such, the act of commemoration is inherently *partial*. Memorials are *incomplete* in that they can only make partial selections from the whole cloth of the past. They are *biased* as well, inasmuch as this imperative to cut and abstract leads inevitably to charges of being partial to one side or the other. Thus, memorials bear *partial* witness to the past, calling attention to some portion of the narratives associated with a place, and, in the process, often obscuring other, sometimes competing memories.

While memorial entrepreneurs may aspire to present an unchanging, static version of history, these hopes are rendered vain and untenable in the face of discontinuous, ruptured, and changing interpretations of the past. In the course of modernity's creative cycle of destruction and rebirth, some moments of the past are favored and others are obscured. Nevertheless, as recent events in Selma so ably demonstrate, it is difficult for competing memories to erase completely or utterly transcend one another. In effect, they need each other. If one ceases to exist, the other will not long endure as a vital, relevant memorial. Given the necessity of antagonistic pairings in crafting identities—

what would black mean without white?—antagonistic memorial narratives are bound in dynamic tension, a dynamism that is enacted on and through the cultural landscape. On the one hand, memorials are weighty artifacts that appear authoritatively to encase history. On the other hand, the unhinged condition of their meaning renders them fundamentally indeterminate. It is this contrast between the permanent and the fleeting that gives memorials their political value. They extend the contradictory promise of "remembering" history while in practice providing but fleeting refuge from an onslaught of ongoing interpretation.

Conclusion

Intersections

Montgomery, Alabama—like any city or town—is filled with intersecting streets. Among them is the junction of Jefferson Davis Avenue, named for the lone president of the Confederate States of America, and Rosa Parks Avenue, named in honor of the woman whose polite refusal to relinquish her seat sparked the most famous campaign for racial equality in the United States. Their intersection symbolizes the powerful convergence of historical memory and identity that characterize Montgomery as the birthplace of two intertwined American revolutions—the Civil War and the Civil Rights Movement. Indeed, a city block from the capitol building where Jefferson Davis was sworn into office is the Dexter Avenue Baptist Church, where Martin Luther King, Jr. served as pastor and led the year-long boycott that desegregated the city's buses in 1956. A decade later, the victorious Voting Rights March paraded past the church on its way to the state capitol. Masses of tourists will soon make the same journey along the heritage trail that marks the march's route from Selma to Montgomery. At the culmination of the march, Movement luminaries addressed the crowd from the building's steps. Movement folklore has it that George Wallace removed the bronze star marking the very spot where Jefferson Davis took his oath, lest it be trampled upon by the likes of a Nobel Peace Prize winner. Nearby, Maya Lin's *Civil Rights Memorial* stands in quiet witness to lives lost in the struggle. Historic markers note that the street linking the capitol and King's former church played host to the city's slave market and the first public performance of "Dixie." Thirty minutes by car to the west are the rolling fields of Lowndes County, in which SNCC (Student Nonviolent Coordinating Committee) activists organized the original Black Panther Party. Thirty minutes in the opposite direction are the manicured lawns and studious buildings that constitute Booker T. Washington's legacy at Tuskegee Institute. The sheer density of sites related to the quest for citizenship in a multiracial society makes Montgomery's memorial landscape a rich mosaic of complexly nested tiles.

Viewed from the perspective of cultural geography, the streets named in honor of Rosa

Parks and Jefferson Davis express the common desire to (re)shape the built environment to celebrate a particular view of the past. That Davis should be commemorated in a Southern city is not surprising. Between 1880 and 1920, Confederate partisans recast the South's memorial landscape in their image.[1] The statuary and plaques that dominate the capitol's grounds attest to their fruitful labor. That Parks should be commemorated as well is becoming less surprising as the Movement's legacy is increasingly enshrined on the landscape. It is, however, extraordinary that streets laden with such symbolically heavy and diametrically opposed loads should intersect. Their intersection bespeaks the complexity of Montgomery's cultural landscape and the multitude of stories associated with it: one icon fought to leave the nation while the other fought to be included fully in it. Now they are both enshrined in the city's collective memory. How are we to understand this scene? Assuming that these street signs did not appear by chance, what does their intersection suggest about the city? Several possible interpretations come to mind.

- Might the intersection allude to a willingness on the part of the city's residents to recognize the complexity of the past? Rather than trying to ignore or to sanitize portions deemed offensive, Montgomery is seemingly embracing all elements of its past. To do so would certainly give substance to William Faulkner's quip that the past is not dead; it's not even past. It would also be refreshingly candid. In America's winner-take-all political culture, the abiding juxtaposition of opposing viewpoints might suggest a measure of understanding and respect sorely lacking in other facets of public life. The state's ongoing efforts to remake the capitol grounds to acknowledge the enduring presence of African Americans suggests this willingness.

- Less hopefully, perhaps it is also true that the situation represents an armed truce in which ideological foes have squared-off, bent—literally at right angles—on having their way. Unable to dominate the (re)presentation of the history and unwilling to appreciate the messy, rich diversity of the past, the opposing parties have settled into an uncomfortable segregation of the past into black and white histories.

- More cynically, could it be the case that the city recognizes that there is money to be made by displaying its history? Admittedly, this is an uncomfortable line of reasoning, inasmuch as it reduces commemoration to a single, base motive: lucre. That said, what better way to capture an increasing market share in the heritage tourism industry than to have something "historical" for whites and blacks?

- How do passersby react to the scene? Interviews and surveys would certainly indicate that some feel pride while some feel apathy and mourn what they feel is a lost cause. Others might find one or both streets offensive. All of these reactions presuppose a degree of historical consciousness, but what happens in its absence? Memorials are typically meant to broadcast an unequivocal lesson to all who behold them. They are produced to shape the future by literally—if futilely—placing memory beyond time's ravaging effect. All plans are undone if the names mean nothing to the average viewer. Might it be the case that the intersection's historical significance is lost on most passersby, their appetite for history dulled by a youthful diet of disconnected historical dates and a parade of (in)famous characters? Those bold enough to propose a memorial must confront the inevitable fact that, once in place, memorials can be ignored.

Of course, this short list is only a beginning. It is neither exhaustive nor are its contents mutually exclusive: one interpretation of a landscape does not preclude the possibility of another meaninig. A thorough examination of the historical record and current opinion might shrink or enlarge this list's content. Without corroborating scholarship (from archival research, surveys, and interviews) the list remains little more than speculation. Such scholarship requires time and access, neither of which is easily granted to the traveling public. There are, however, habits of mind that can enrich the experience of visiting places of collective memory. The principles of interpretation for memorial landscapes that we offer below are intended as aids in the development of these habits. The inspiration for these principles and their attendant questions lies with Peirce Lewis, a cultural geographer, master teacher, and trenchant critic of the American scene. Lewis's attention to the ways that places both reflect and reproduce how people live is exemplary. His articles, book chapters, and now classic book—*New Orleans: The Making of an Urban Landscape, Third Edition*—are required reading for those who hanker to explore the cultural landscape.[2]

Lewis encouraged his students to interpret landscapes, such as the intersection of Parks and Davis, as one would a book: as cultural artifacts that at once reflect and reproduce social norms. In a seminal essay, "Axioms for Reading the Landscape: Some Guides to the American Scene," Lewis enunciated seven maxims for making sense of the built environment. Guided by these maxims, ephemera, such as yard ornaments, fast-food restaurants, and junkyards, become valuable data for making sense of how Americans relate to the land and to one another. "Our human landscape," Lewis writes, "is our unwitting autobiography, reflecting our tastes, our values, our aspirations, and even our fears, in tangible, visible form."[3] Lewis offered his axioms as a helpmeet in what he understood to be the intellectual equivalent of parsing a sentence: "What we needed were some guides to help us read the landscape, just as rules of grammar sometimes help guide us through some particularly convoluted bit of syntax."[4] Lewis developed this line of reasoning—the landscape-as-text—describing landscapes as "clues" to decoding the intricacies of culture: its morphology, diffusion, and regional variation. He championed the notion that there are no irrelevant landscapes. Even the smallest, meanest element deserves inspection as evidence of care—or the lack thereof—on the part of its "authors." Finally, he warned that landscape interpretation is difficult, typically obscured by the landscape's origins in a distant time and place, technology, and taste. In response, he prescribed the analytic power of thoughtful observation and resourceful scholarship.[5]

Lewis proffered his axioms in hopes of breaking the monopoly enjoyed by grand facades and steepled cathedrals over observers of the built environment. He urged all who would listen to pay attention to the ordinary stuff that characterizes the vast majority of landscapes. As our "unwitting" biography, he felt that ordinary things reflect our tastes and prejudices more candidly than self-consciously "serious" landscapes. Thus, at least on the face of it, our focus on civil rights memorials amounts to an intellectual sin in the Lewisian catechism of landscape interpretation. And, were it not for the peculiar situation of memorials, we might agree. As items in the landscape, however, memorials are at once extraordinary and ordinary. In their monumental form, they are exceptional, since the political and economic capital required to raise such proud towers is scarce indeed. Yet they are common in the sense alluded to above: most of the time—and there are important exceptions—memorials drift into the same oblivion to which we daily consign the vast majority of visual stimuli that bombard us. It needn't be thus. Memorial landscapes—every bit as much as chain-link fences, blue highways, and three-car garages—bestow cultural insight upon close inspection. Close inspection—embodied in thoughtful preparation before a trip, careful observation throughout, and critical inquiry in its wake—is the antidote for the twin scourges of heritage tourism: harried "trophy" hunting excursions in search of "important" sites and its all-too-frequent companion, the passive acceptance of memorials at face value. In the place of this bland, unsatisfying fare, close inspection of the Lewisian sort can transform passive heritage tourism into an active engagement with collective memory. We conclude with these principles and questions in the hopes of enabling your own investigations into the production and consumption of civil rights memorials.

Three Principles and Thirty Questions

In the course of clearing new intellectual ground, Peirce Lewis emphasized the necessity of discovering the origins of everyday landscapes.[6] A subsequent generation of scholars—led by geographers such as Jim and Nancy Duncan, Denis Cosgrove, Don Mitchell, and Peter Jackson—has labored to extend and deepen the Lewisian landscape-as-text metaphor, carefully (re)reading landscapes in order to identify the interests served and denied by landscape "authors," the "texts" they produce, and the ways various "readers" interact with those texts.[7] The following principles and questions—inspired by geographers J. P. Jones III and Wolfgang Natter—reflect the manner in which cultural geographers study memorial landscapes as open-ended, symbolic systems, paying close attention to the complex interactions among author, artifact, and audience.[8]

Memorial landscapes can be interpreted like a "text."

A memorial landscape can be examined as if it is an odd sort of book in which each page reflects the handiwork of many authors. Like words inscribed on a page, different stories are made manifest in the landscape. Varying in their particulars but united by common themes of valor, loss, and fidelity, memorials are intended to be "read," to convey a story into the future. Of course, not all texts are equally endowed. Some enjoy extensive promotion while others languish for want of attention. Making sense out of the interplay of authorial intention and an audience's reception begins with careful observation of the artifact itself.[9] The questions below seek to clarify the relationship among the parts and the whole, and among the text and the context, that condition memorials:

1. How did you learn about this memorial? Through word-of-mouth or via mass media? Who promotes this site? The news media? The local Chamber of Commerce? Similarly, how did find your way to the site? Was the route marked in an official manner or did you have to know what you were looking for? Did you have the option of using public transportation to get here? Is the memorial part of a city's established tourism circuit? Can you infer a relationship between the memorial's message and the communication channels promoting it?

2. What kind of neighborhood did you travel through to get here? What surrounds the memorial? Interstates and warehouses? Abandoned apartment blocks? A bustling business district? Gentrified lofts and condos? Would you feel comfortable walking around the neighborhood? Could you afford to live here?

3. To what degree is this memorial connected to its environs? Is there any advertising for other historical sites in the area? Are there bicycle trails and walking paths? Does this memorial invite you to explore the immediate surroundings? Or is it walled off from its neighbors?

4. How prominent are commercial activities on and near the site? How does the presence of vendors and shops affect your experience? Likewise, who benefits

from this memorial? Do local restaurants and shops appear to prosper? Who bears the inevitable costs of increased traffic, noise, and litter?

5. How is the memorial's space organized? For instance, how does the site's layout influence the direction and pace of your experience? Is it subdivided into different kinds of thematic spaces (such as contemplative, conversational, commercial)? Or is it more free-form and less programmed? Does it engage senses beyond the visual? Does it invite you to linger?

6. There are many different ways to record our position in time and space: clock and compass, diary and map, calendar and milepost. Metaphorically, how does this memorial mark time and space? For instance, does this memorial parse time into centuries or seasons? Whereas centuries march into the future like an ascending arrow, seasons cycle through alternating periods of death and rebirth. Likewise, if this memorial was a weathervane, would it be facing into or out of the wind?

7. Think about the scope of the memorial. If it was a map, how much "territory" would it cover? Does it recall a very local, particular event? Or does it claim to be timeless and universal? How does it connect, if at all, to related struggles elsewhere and at other times?

8. Memories are stored in a host of places, including attics, cemeteries, jewel boxes, scrapbooks, and dreams. Of what kind of repository does this memorial most remind you? Similarly, we recall the past via different media, such as history textbooks, dances, home video, digital images, and music. Which of these formats is this memorial like? Which do you find most pleasing?

9. Suppose this memorial had a "center of gravity," a core theme it promised to deliver. Where is it? Typically, the most valued themes are placed in the front, at the center, and on top as opposed to those things relegated to the back, down low, and off to the margin. In like fashion, size and color can reflect value judgments. Having located the "fulcrum," who or what do you find there?

10. Does this memorial remind you of other historic sites you've visited? If not, how does it differ? If the Movement itself marked a radical break with the past, should its memorials do the same?

Like a text, memorial landscapes are "authored."

Typically, memorials are authored by multiple parties. Often it is the case that these parties agree on little more than it being right, and they meet to erect a memorial. Its location, form, and content, however, remain matters of great debate. The odd union of local businesses and civil rights activists enjoined across the South to commemorate the Movement offers a case in point. Whatever their motives, the authors have an abiding stake in the place. For some, this stake may be economic: Alabama Power and Light is bound to its present locale. As a result, it has a ready rationale to improve "Bombingham's" tarnished image. For others, the memorial impulse reflects a desire to intervene in the politics of a place, to recall what has happened, and, above all, to create a future legacy. That said, not all memorial "authors" have equal access to the "text," inasmuch as some stories are muted and suppressed while others appear front-and-center.

1. Who claims responsibility for this memorial? Were they the winners or losers of the conflict in question? In light of the memorial's core themes, what do they want you to remember? Is there anything they want you to forget?

2. Is this memorial the outcome of local initiative? How much political and economic capital did its producers wield? To what extent, if any, did they draw on national or international support?

3. From what source(s) does this memorial's authority issue? How do its authors seek to persuade you that their account of the past is right? Is the site hallowed by dint of sacrifice? By a grand size and a sweeping layout? By folk authenticity? Has it been endorsed by celebrities and dignitaries? Inescapably, even the plainest descriptions—"such-and-such happened here on this date"—embody a rhetorical appeal, even to the disinterested reporter. How does this site's design intend to persuade you?

4. To whom do the authors direct their message? Does the memorial's orientation relative to the city's social geography provide any clues? Does the memorial issue a summons to the city's power brokers or does it celebrate their efforts? Does it offer inspiration to the poor and downtrodden or ignore them? Does

it look beyond the city altogether, perhaps toward the nation or humanity as a whole? Do the authors claim international importance or is the memorial's reputation wholly local?

5. If this memorial could talk, what kind of accent would it have? Would everyone be able to understand it? Would it harmonize or rhapsodize? Would it speak in riddles and poetic verse or something official-sounding, like an entry from the encyclopedia?

6. In light of its "accent," can you guess the background of the site's producers? Whose "voice" predominates? How might things be done differently? What difference does it make to you?

7. Again, supposing the memorial could talk, would its tone be that of the disinterested reporter or the triumphal partisan? Would it lecture you or start up a conversation? Would it dwell on the past or the future? Would it whisper or shout?

8. Similarly, is this memorial designed to put forth answers or questions? And if you asked a question of it, how would it respond to your queries? With answers or questions in return? Would it say the same thing to everyone, regardless of their background?

9. If this memorial was a film, who did the authors cast in the leading role? Who plays the good guy? Who is the villain? Are women included? Who is pictured leading? Who is pictured sitting? Who exists as an individual? Who is lumped together in a mass?

10. What kind of ending have the authors given this memorial? Do you think they saw the memorial as a beginning—perhaps a nursery—or as an end, like a mausoleum? Did they design the place to commemorate loss or achievement or both? To what extent is the Movement represented as "won"? What, if anything, is left unfinished? Is it morning or night for the Movement? Is it facing uphill or downhill?

Like a text memorial landscapes are "read" by multiple audiences.

By reflecting *and* refracting cultural norms, memorials contribute to continuity *and* to change in a society. While memorials reflect the interests of their authors, they are rendered silent in the absence of an audience. No memorial speaks for itself; each one is dependent upon its audience to voice—or betray—its vision of the past and future. And, just as with a book, "readers" will (re)act differently to what is ostensibly the same story. As a result, a landscape's intended message may slip, take on unforeseen nuances, or even be contradicted outright. No memorial landscape can be considered complete in any final sense; each is susceptible to ongoing interpretation. As such, memorials are places at which cultural norms are reinforced or challenged, reproduced or altered via an audience's reactions. These reactions come in many forms, ranging from the ways visitors behave on site to the stories they recount in the wake of their visit.

1. How are you supposed to behave at this place? What kinds of behavioral cues are embedded in the landscape? Do benches and water suggest quiet contemplation? Do stairs and alter-like risers lend a sense of anticipation? Does anything hint at the possibility of noisy expression or a communal experience?[10]

2. Who visits this memorial? In what ways is the audience mixed in terms of age, race, class, and gender? Do different audiences interact with the site and one another in different ways? Are children welcome? Is the memorial handicap accessible? Is it multilingual?

3. Is there any evidence that locals frequent this place (such as the availability of guest registers, photocopied handbills, meeting rooms for gatherings, picnic benches, and bus stops)? Are there skateboarders or panhandlers or counterprotestors? What sort of alternative uses might this memorial support?

4. How do people treat this site? Has it been trashed with graffiti or litter? Who carries out the work of cleaning and maintaining this place? Are they visible or hidden? Does this memorial celebrate their efforts in any way? If the site is not kept up, what does this suggest about the present condition of its message?

5. What can you infer from the posture and disposition of the people around you? How are they "reading" this place? Does their behavior suggest the presence of something sacred? A carefree holiday? Boredom? Is anyone outraged or offended by this memorial? If not, is it so bland as to be meaningless?

6. Does this memorial reflect your experience? Conversely, what aspects does it ignore or deny? Imagine a person who is your "opposite" in terms of race, class, gender, nationality, and such. How might he or she interpret this site? Could the site be changed to include their beliefs and perspectives? What would this do to the memorial?

7. How would you go about studying reactions to this public space? What questions would you ask visitors? What kinds of places would you compare it to? How different is it, say, from the Liberty Bell or even a scene at Disneyland?

8. Does the memorial inspire you or leave you feeling lost? How would you change this site, if at all?

9. Will you return to this site? Why or why not? Do you think your grandchildren will visit this place? How might their experience differ from yours? Does this memorial have an implicit "expiration date" after which it will no longer be relevant? Under what conditions might it become obsolete or kept current?

10. Is this a site of ongoing activism? Are there signs that some people are trying to align their cause with this site? Have other parties attached their symbols and messages onto this site? Or is it largely ignored as a target for symbolic accretion?

We offer these principles and questions by way of inviting you to make sense out of the relationship (is there harmony or tension?) between the extraordinary and ordinary, stasis and change, intention and interpretation that characterize civil rights memorial landscapes. The cultural landscape is all around us, and every bit of it reveals some things and obscures others. Awareness of the memorial landscape is an acquired taste, and its mastery is years in the making. That said, its rudiments are accessible to all. When we slow down and ask serious questions about the stories placed before us, we honor those whose pursuit of free and open access to the means of representation made these sites possible in the first place.

Notes

Introduction

1. A description of the Chattanooga street-naming struggle can also be found in Derek H. Alderman, "Naming Streets after Martin Luther King, Jr.: No Easy Road," in Richard Schein, ed., *Race and Landscape in the United States* (New York: Routledge Press, 2006), 213–36. Thanks to Ron Foresta for making us aware of the events in Chattanooga.

2. Pat Wilcox, "New Request Made to Rename Ninth Street for Late Dr. King," *Chattanooga Times*, January 21, 1981: B2.

3. Ibid.

4. Pat Wilcox, "Unity Asked in Street Name Change," *Chattanooga Times*, March 25, 1981: B1.

5. Pat Wilcox, "City Won't Rename Street, Designates Memorial Area," *Chattanooga Times*, April 8, 1981: A1.

6. Pat Wilcox, "Key Would Halt Project if Street Not Renamed," *Chattanooga Times*, April 3, 1981: B2.

7. Dave Flessner, "Key Vows to Continue Name Fight," *Chattanooga Times*, April 9, 1981: A1.

8. Gary Fine, *Difficult Reputations: Collective Memories of the Evil, Inept, and Controversial* (Chicago: University of Chicago Press, 2001).

9. Randall Gray, "Balking on 9th St. Termed 'Asinine,'" *Chattanooga News-Free Press*, April 5, 1981: A1.

10. Pat Wilcox, "King Boulevard Signs Removed; Coalition Will Continue Petitions," *Chattanooga Times*, April 21, 1981: B1.

11. Jeff Powell, "Blacks 'Rename' Ninth Street," *Chattanooga News-Free Press*, April 19, 1981: A1.

12. Ibid.

13. Ibid.

14. Pat Wilcox, "City Reverses, Renames Ninth Street for King," *Chattanooga Times*, July 15, 1981: A1; and Pat Wilcox, "City Pays Tribute to M. L. King Jr., Street Dedicated," *Chattanooga Times*, January 16, 1982: A1.

15. Pat Wilcox, "Reaction to Ninth Street Renaming Mixed at City Hall," *Chattanooga Times*, July 16, 1981: A1.

16. Jonathan Tilove, *Along Martin Luther King: Travels on Black America's Main Street* (New York: Random House, 2003); and Pat Wilcox, "Key Calls Change in Read House Address Racism," *Chattanooga Times*, January 16, 1982: A1.

17. Joseph Tilden Rhea, *Race Pride and American Identity* (Cambridge: Harvard University Press, 1997).

18. Gary Fine, op. cit.

19. Pat Wilcox, "City Reverses, Renames Ninth Street for King," *Chattanooga Times*, July 15, 1981: A1.

20. Wilbur Zelinsky, *Nation into State: The Shifting Symbolic Foundations of American Nationalism* (Chapel Hill: University of North Carolina Press, 1988).

21. Pat Wilcox, "Blacks Say 9th Street Name to Go," *Chattanooga Times*, April 4, 1981: A1.

22. For example, see Steven D. Hoelscher, "Making Place, Making Race: Performances of Whiteness in the Jim Crow South," *Annals of the Association of American Geographers* 93 (2003): 657–86.

23. Roy Rosenzweig and David Thelen, *Presence of the Past: Popular Uses of History in American Life* (New York: Columbia University Press, 1998).

24. Street name data were collected from *American Business Disc*, www.melissadata.com, and www.mapblast.com by Derek Alderman, Matthew Mitchelson, and Christopher McPhilamy.

25. School name data were collected from *Common Core of Data, 2002–2003*, a publication of the National Center for Educational Statistics, U.S. Department of Education.

26. Roger W. Stump, "Toponymic Commemoration of National Figures: The Cases of Kennedy and King," *Names* 36 (1988), No. 3/4: 203–16.

27. Derek H. Alderman, "School Names as Cultural Arenas: The Naming of U.S. Public Schools after Martin Luther King, Jr.," *Urban Geography* 23 (2002), No. 7: 601–26.

28. Jim Gray, "King Drive Street Name Voted Down," *Atlanta Constitution*, April 15, 1976: A1.

29. Derek H. Alderman and Owen J. Dwyer, "Putting Memory in its Place: The Politics of Commemoration in the American South," in Donald Janelle, Barney Warf, and Kathy Hansen, eds., *WorldMinds: Geographical Perspectives on 100 Problems*, (Dordrecht, Netherlands: Kluwer Academic Publishers, 2004), 55–60.

30. Nikki Burns, "Stokes Says He Will Continue to Burn State Flag in Protest," *Mississippi Link* (online edition), April 24, 2003: n.p. Last accessed May 2007 at http://www.mississippilink.net/.

31. Brian Graham, G. J. Ashworth, and J. E. Tunbridge, *A Geography of Heritage* (New York: Oxford University Press, 2000), 5.

32. Kirk Savage, *Standing Soldiers, Kneeling Slaves: Race, War, and Monument in Nineteenth-Century America* (Princeton: Princeton University Press, 1997), 135.

33. Maoz Azaryahu, "The Power of Commemorative Street Names," *Environment and Planning D: Society and Space* 14 (1996), 311–30.

34. James Loewen, *Lies Across America: What Our Historic Sites Get Wrong* (New York: The New Press, 1999), 214.

35. Larry Boulard, "New Orleans Battles Over a Monument," *Christian Science Monitor*, April 19, 1993: 12.

36. Geographers' thoughts about the cultural landscape have generated a voluminous number of studies of which the following may serve as an entry point for the interested reader: Philip L. Wagner and Marvin W. Mikesell, eds., *Readings in Cultural Geography* (Chicago: University of Chicago Press, 1962); Kenneth E. Foote, Kent Mathewson, and Peter J. Hugill, eds., *Re-Reading Cultural Geography* (Austin: University of Texas Press, 1994); Doreen Massey, *Space, Place, and Gender* (Minneapolis: University of Minnesota Press, 1994); Don Mitchell, *Cultural Geography: A Critical Introduction* (Malden, Mass.: Blackwell Publishers, 2000);

Kay Anderson, Mona Domosh, Nigel Thrift, and Steve Pile, eds., *Handbook of Cultural Geography* (London: Sage, 2003); James S. Duncan, Nuala C. Johnson, and Richard H. Schein, eds., *A Companion to Cultural Geography* (Malden, Mass.: Blackwell Publishers, 2004); and Brett Wallach, *Understanding the Cultural Landscape* (New York: Guilford Press, 2004).

37. Rosenzweig and Thelen, op. cit., 18.

38. Loewen, op. cit.; and Townsend Davis, *Weary Feet, Rested Souls: A Guided History of the Civil Rights Movement* (New York: W. W. Norton and Company, 1998).

39. Kenneth E. Foote, *Shadowed Ground: America's Landscapes of Violence and Tragedy* (Austin: University of Texas Press, 1997), 33.

40. Dell Upton, "Commemorating the Civil Rights Movement," *Design Book Review* 40 (Fall 1999): 22–33; see, also, Catherine Howett, "Kelly Ingram Park: A Place of Revolution and Reconciliation," *Landscape Architecture* 83 (March 1993): 34–35.

41. Upton, op. cit.

42. Melvin Dixon, "The Black Writer's Use of Memory," in Geneviève Fabre and Robert O'Meally, eds., *History and Memory in African-American Culture* (New York: Oxford University Press, 1994), 18–27.

43. Renee Romano and Leigh Radford, eds., *The Civil Rights Movement in American Memory* (Athens: University of Georgia Press, 2006).

44. Jim Carrier, *A Traveler's Guide to the Civil Rights Movement* (Orlando, Fl.: Harcourt Books, 2004); and Davis, op. cit.

45. Foote, op. cit.; Arnold R. Alanen and Robert Z. Melnick, eds., *Preserving Cultural Landscapes in America* (Baltimore: The Johns Hopkins University Press, in association with the Center for American Places, 2000); Gail Lee Dubrow and Jennifer B. Goodman, eds., *Restoring Women's History through Historic Preservation* (Baltimore: The Johns Hopkins University Press, in association with the Center for American Places, 2003); Steven D. Hoelscher, *Heritage on Stage: The Invention of Ethnic Place in America's Little Switzerland* (Madison: University of Wisconsin Press, 1998); Sanford Levinson, *Written in Stone: Public Monuments in Changing Societies* (Durham: Duke University Press, 1998); Loewen, op. cit.; David Lowenthal, *The Past is a Foreign Country* (Cambridge: Cambridge University Press, 1985); Simon

Schama, *Landscape and Memory* (New York: Vintage Books, 1995); and James E. Young, *The Texture of Memory* (New Haven: Yale University Press, 1993).

Chapter One

1. These ideas are gracefully developed in Kirk Savage, *Standing Soldiers, Kneeling Slaves: Race, War, and Monuments in Niteteenth-Centruy America* (Princeton: Princeton University Press, 1997).

2. W. Fitzhugh Brundage, *The Southern Past: A Clash of Race and Memory* (Cambridge: Harvard University Press, 2005) 60; see, also, W. Fitzhugh Brundage, *Where These Memories Grow: History, Memory, and Southern Identity* (Chapel Hill: University of North Carolina Press, 2000). For a consideration of African-American commemoration in particular, see Kathleen Ann Clark, *Festivals of Freedom: Memory and Meaning in African American Emancipation Celebrations, 1808–1915* (Amherst and Boston: University of Massachusetts Press, 2003); and Kathleen Ann Clark, *Defining Moments: African American Commemoration and Political Culture in the South, 1863–1913* (Chapel Hill: University of North Carolina Press, 2005).

3. Brundage (2005), op. cit.

4. Glenn T. Eskew, "From Civil War to Civil Rights: Selling Alabama as Heritage Tourism," *International Journal of Hospitality & Tourism Administration* 2 (2001), No. 3/4: 201–14.

5. Carol Mueller, "Ella Baker and the Origins of 'Participatory Democracy,'" in Vicki L. Crawford, Jacqueline A. Rouse, and Barbara Woods, eds., *Women in the Civil Rights Movement: Trailblazers and Torchbearers, 1941–1965* (New York: Carlson Publishing, Inc.; 1990), 51–70; and Charles Payne, "Ella Baker and Models of Social Change," *Signs: Journal of Women in Culture and Society* 14 (1989): 885–99.

6. Cynthia S. Brown, *Ready from Within: Septima Clark and the Civil Rights Movement* (Trenton, N.J.: Africa World Press, 1990); and Grace Jordan McFadden, "Septima P. Clark and the Struggle for Human Rights," in Crawford et al., eds., op. cit., 85–98.

7. Mueller, op. cit., 51.

8. Clayborne Carson, "Civil Rights Reform and the Black Freedom Struggle," in

Charles W. Eagles, ed., *The Civil Rights Movement in America*, (Jackson: University Press of Mississippi, 1986), 19–32.

9. Dave Murray, "Naming Schools After Civil-Rights Leaders Would Make Important Statement, Administrators Say," *Grand Rapids Press*, August 29, 2005: A1.

10. Abigail Jordan, *To Honor our Forbearers: The Trials and Tribulations of Building the African American Monument in Savannah, Georgia* (unpublished manuscript, n.d.), 8.

11. Ibid, 9.

12. National Public Radio, "Residents of Savannah in Disagreement," *All Things Considered*, April 30, 2001.

13. Robert R. Weyeneth, "Historical Preservation and the Civil Rights Movement," *CRM Bulletin* 18 (1995): 6–8; see, also, Robert R. Weyeneth, "Historical Preservation and the Civil Rights Movement of the 1950s and 1960s: Identifying, Preserving, and Interpreting the Architecture of Liberation: A Report to Preservation Agencies." (The published report is available by contacting the author.) A new book, however, has been released: Charles E. Cobb Jr., *On the Road to Freedom: A Guided Tour of the Civil Rights Trail* (Chapel Hill, N.C.: Algonquin Books, 2008).

14. Derek H. Alderman, *Creating a New Geography of Memory in the South: The Politics of (Re)Naming Streets after Martin Luther King Jr.* (unpublished dissertation: University of Georgia, 1998).

15. Marianna Warner, *Monuments and Maidens: The Allegory of the Female Form* (London: Weidenfield and Nicolson, 1985); and Jan Monk, "Gender in the Landscape: Expressions of Power and Meaning," in Kay Anderson and Faye Gale, eds., *Inventing Places: Studies in Cultural Geography* (Melbourne: Longman Cheshire, 1992), 123–38.

16. Diane Barthel, "Getting in Touch with History: The Role of Historic Preservation in Shaping Collective Memories," *Qualitative Sociology* 19 (1996), No. 3: 345–64.

17. Owen J. Dwyer, *Memorial Landscapes Dedicated to the Civil Rights Movement* (unpublished dissertation: University of Kentucky, 2000).

18. Ibid.

19. Ibid. This kind of age (or generational) distinction was also prevelant in the

Democratic presidential primaries of 2008 in which Barack Obama consistently appealed to voters under forty-five years old and Hillary Clinton to those above forty-five.

20. Frederick Allen, "Fowler Fights for King Drive," *Atlanta Constitution*, April 4, 1976: 2A.

21. Bernard J. Armada, "Memorial Agon: An Interpretive Tour of the National Civil Rights Museum," *Southern Communication Journal* 63 (1998): 235–43; and John Paul Jones III, "The Street Politics of Jackie Smith," in Gary Bridge and Sophie Watson, eds., *The Blackwell Companion to the City* (Oxford: Blackwell Publishers, 2000), 448–59.

22. Eileen Loh-Harrist, "Vigil of a Lifetime: Jacqueline Smith's Views are as Concrete as the Sidewalk Before the Civil Rights Museum," *The Memphis Flyer*, November 19–25, 1998: 14–17.

Chapter Two

1. Street name data are available online through *American Business Disc*, www.melissadata.com, and www.mapblast.com.

2. Dan E. Way, "Rosa Parks' Name Appears Around the Country," *Gannett News Service*, October 25, 2005: ARC; Ellen Gedalius, "Tampa Floats Idea to Rename Street for Civil Rights Heroine," *Tampa Tribune*, November 3, 2005: Nation/World section, 4; Jacob Santini, "Rename Road for Rosa Parks; W. Jordan Has No Policy," *Salt Lake Tribune*, November 16, 2005: D3; and *Associated Press State & Local Wire*, "Senate Votes to Rename Portion of I-96 in Honor of Rosa Parks," November 30, 2005: n.p.

3. Erin Haines, "Suburban Atlanta's 'Tara Boulevard' Could Be Gone With the Wind," *Associated Press State & Local Wire*, November 17, 2005: n.p.

4. Lynne Jensen, "School Names Reflect New Era; Washington Put on Casualty List," *Times-Picayune*, October 24, 1997: A1; and Chris Gray, "Push on to Rename Schools," *Times-Picayune*, December 2, 1997: B3.

5. Although our book focuses on civil rights memorials in the United States, it is worth mentioning that the commemoration of Dr. King and the Movement is a global phenomenon. Less than a week after King's assassination, the city council of Haarlem, The Netherlands, voted to name a street for the civil rights leader. See "Other Harlem Giving King's Name to Street," *Chicago Tribune*, April 10, 1968: 2. Other international commemorative renamings for King include named streets in Belgium, Israel, and Italy; plazas and squares in Russia, Brazil, and India; and schools in Panama and Cameroon.

6. Jonathan Tilove, *Along Martin Luther King: Travels on Black America's Main Street* (New York: Random House, 2003).

7. "Vote to Name City Street in Honor of King," *Chicago Tribune*, July 30, 1968: B8.

8. Tilove, op. cit.

9. Matthew Mitchelson, Derek H. Alderman, and Jeff Popke, "Branded: The Economic Geographies of MLK Streets," *Social Science Quarterly* 88 (2007), No. 1: 120–45.

10. Bond Brungard, "Newburgh Street Named for Civil Rights Leader," *Poughkeepsie Journal*, August 29, 2005: B2.

11. Taylor Branch, *Pillar of Fire: America in the King Years, 1963–65* (New York: Simon & Schuster, 1998).

12. James R. Ralph, Jr., "Home Truths: Dr. King and The Chicago Freedom Movement," *American Visions* 9 (1994), No. 4: 30–33; Tilove, op. cit.; and Wallace Best, "'The Right Achieved and the Wrong Way Conquered': J. H. Jackson, Martin Luther King, Jr., and the Conflict Over Civil Rights," *Religion and American Culture* 16 (2006), No. 2: 195–226.

13. Tilove, op. cit.

14. "Street's Name Switch Riles Portland Residents, Fierce Public Backlash to Avenue Named after Martin Luther King Jr.," *Seattle Times*, March 4, 1990: D5.

15. Peter Scott, "Failure to Name Street to Honor MLK May Bring Boycott," *Atlanta Journal and Constitution*, November 28, 1992: B9.

16. Craig Pittman, "King's Fight Still in the Streets: Renaming Roads Incites Controversy," *St. Petersburg Times*, April 23, 1990: B1.

17. Marilyn Bellemore, "M.L.K. Day Does Not Fit Patriotic Holiday Policy, Munroe

Says," *The Standard Times* (online), November 17, 2005: n.p. Last accessed May 2007 at www.nkstandrardtimes.com.

18. "Citizen Comments Sent to City in Reference to Renaming Airport Road" (Chapel Hill, N.C.: City Hall Records, 2004).

19. Michael Eric Dyson, *I May Not Get There With You: The True Martin Luther King, Jr.* (New York: Free Press, 2000), 6.

20. Derek H. Alderman, "Street Names as Memorial Arenas: The Reputational Politics of Commemorating Martin Luther King, Jr. in a Georgia County," *Historical Geography* 30 (2002): 99–120.

21. Susan Smith Richardson, "Austin's Street Fighting," *Austin American-Statesman*, August 30, 1998: H2; and Norma Martin, "Life Along King's Streets," *Austin American-Statesman*, January 18, 1999: E1.

22. Melvin McLawhorn, opening remarks for "Along Martin Luther King: Travels on Black America's Main Streets," public presentation by Jonathan Tilove at East Carolina University, February 10, 2005.

23. Brenda Yarbrough, "Street Honoring King Leads to City Dump," *Atlanta Constitution*, October 30, 1992: A3.

24. Keli Dailey, "Streets of MLK Cry Out the Dream is Incomplete," *San Francisco Chronicle*, April 3, 2005: C1.

25. Jim Yardley, "Boulevard of Broken Dreams," *Atlanta Journal and Constitution*, January 14, 1995: A3.

26. Jamie Satterfield, "Taking Back the Streets; Project Safe Neighborhoods Targets MLK-Lined Section as Most Violent Area in Knox," *Knoxville News-Sentinel*, May 19, 2004: A1.

27. Matthew Mitchelson, *The Economic Geography of MLK Streets* (unpublished master's thesis: East Carolina University, 2005).

28. Jennifer Jacobs and Brianna Blake, "Strongest Street in Town," *Des Moines Register*, January 16, 2005: 1B.

29. Derek H. Alderman, "A Street Fit for a King: Naming Places and Commemoration in the American South," *Professional Geographer* 52 (2000), No. 4: 672–84; and Mitchelson, op. cit.

30. Mitchelson, op. cit.

31. Christina Headrick, "NAACP Wants Martin Luther King Jr. Avenue Moved," *St. Petersburg Times*, August 31, 2001: 7; and Adrienne P. Samuels, "Greenwood Avenue Name Deeply Rooted," *Clearwater Times*, January 31, 2005: 1.

32. Donna Hilton, "Wilson Chains Himself to MLK Sign at I-30 Bridge," *Siftings Herald News* (online), February 15, 2005: n.p. Last accessed May 2007 at www.siftingsherald.com.

33. Rick Yencer, "Unity Line Pushes Issue," *The Star Press*, August 10, 2003: 1A.

34. Eli'sa Corley, Jr., "Choose Another Street to Rename in King's Honor (letter to the editor)," *The Daily Leader* (online), March 15, 2005: n.p. Last accessed March 2005 at www.zwire.com.

35. For a fuller discussion of the Athens, Georgia, case, see Derek H. Alderman, "Creating a New Geography of Memory in the South: The (Re)Naming of Streets in Honor of Martin Luther King, Jr," *Southeastern Geographer* 36 (1996), No. 1: 51–69.

36. T. Davis, "Council Rejects MLK Road Proposal," *Danville Register & Bee*, March 6, 2002: 1A.

37. Tilove, op. cit., 122.

38. For general information on the founding of the King National Historic Site, see Charles Rutheiser, *Imagineering Atlanta: The Politics of Place in the City of Dreams* (London: Verso, 1996); Ebba Hierta, "Overcoming the Odds," *National Parks* 70 (1996): 40; and National Park Service, *A Grand Endeavor for a Man with a Dream, The Story of the Martin Luther King, Jr., National Historic Site and Preservation District* (Washington, D.C.: Department of the Interior, 1997).

39. Lucy Lawliss, *Martin Luther King, Jr. National Historic Site Cultural Landscape Report: Birth-Home Block* (Atlanta: National Park Service, Southeast Regional Office, 1995); and Robert Blythe, et al., *Martin Luther King, Jr. National Historic Site Historic Resource Study* (Atlanta: National Park Service, Southeast Regional Office, 1994).

40. Howard Pousner "King Family Plans Disney-like Park," *Atlanta Journal and Constitution*, August 11, 1994: C1; Howard Pousner, "The King Site Fight," *Atlanta Journal and Constitution*, January 21, 1995: B2; and John Blake, "King Week '95: Q & A: Dexter King and Troy Lissimore: Main Figures in King Controversy Discuss

Conflict over District's Future," *Atlanta Journal and Constitution*, January 15, 1995: D4.

41. Mark Sherman, "King Center Dips into Endowment," *Atlanta Journal and Constitution*, February 1, 1995: A1; and Mark Sherman and John Blake, "King Center's Finances: More Federal Funding May Be Difficult," *Atlanta Journal and Constitution*, February 1, 1995: D4.

42. General information on the creation of the Birmingham Civil Rights Institute can be found in Jimmie Lewis Franklin, *Back to Birmingham: Richard Arrington, Jr. and His Times* (Tuscaloosa: University of Alabama Press, 1989); Sandy Coleman, "Birmingham's Civil Rights Institute Presents a Compelling History of the Movement," *Boston Globe*, February 26, 1995: B21; Thomas Cox, *Reflections on a Place of Revolution and Reconciliation: A Brief History of Kelly Ingram Park and the Birmingham Civil Rights District* (Birmingham: Birmingham Civil Rights Institute, 1995); and Glenn T. Eskew, "The Birmingham Civil Rights Institute and the New Ideology of Tolerance," in Renee Romano and Leigh Raiford, eds., *The Civil Rights Movement in American Memory* (Athens: University of Georgia Press, 2006), 28–66.

43. Terry Horne, "Rights Museum Remains a Dream," *Birmingham Post-Herald*, February 14, 1984: 8.

44. "Case Study No. 2333: Intensive Media Campaign Fuels Support for Civil Rights Facility," *PR News*, January 25, 1993: 4–5; see, also, Joe Nabbefeld, "Institute Should Have Strong Impact on City Economy," *The Birmingham News*, November 15, 1992: 14.

45. Roy L. Williams, "Downtown Construction Revitalization Picks Up Zip," *Birmingham News*, January 11, 1998: 27-H; Sherrel Wheeler Stewart, "Residents Protest Neighborhood Plan," *Birmingham News*, January 13, 1999: 2-C; and Anita Debro, "Fountain Heights Demands Action," *Birmingham News*, February 24, 1999: 1-N.

46. For general information on the history of the National Civil Rights Museum, see Wayne Risher, "Museum is Fruition of Dreams of Motel Owner, Many Others," *The Commercial Appeal*, September 21, 1991: special section; Alice Faye Duncan, *The National Civil Rights Museum Celebrates Everyday People* (Memphis: Bridgewater Books, 1995); Kenneth R. Adderly, *Monument on the Mississippi: Background, Development, and the Rising Significance of the National Civil Rights Museum*

(unpublished master's thesis: University of Memphis, 1997); and Kenneth E. Foote, *Shadowed Ground: America's Landscapes of Violence and Tragedy* (Austin: University of Texas Press, 1997).

47. The museum continues to make the headlines, as critics recently pressed their demands for changes in the museum's management, including a desire for more African Americans on the board of directors. See Woody Baird, of the Associated Press, "Civil Rights Museum critics rally for new management," *The Tuscaloosa News*, December 9, 2007: 5B.

48. The story of the National Voting Rights Museum is told in Rose Sanders, *Sharing the Torch: A Mini History of the Voting Rights Movement* (Selma, Al.: National Voting Rights Museum and Institute, 1997).

49. Stephen G. N. Tuck, *Beyond Atlanta: The Struggle for Racial Equality in Georgia, 1940–1980* (Athens: University of Georgia Press, 2001).

Chapter Three

1. Kenneth E. Foote, *Shadowed Ground: America's Landscapes of Violence and Tragedy* (Austin: University of Texas Press, 1997).

2. Monica Davey, "Chicago Divided Over Proposal to Honor a Slain Black Panther," *New York Times*, March 5, 2006: 18.

3. Fran Spielman, "Cop Leader: 'You've got to be kidding': City Committee Wants to Name Street after Slain Black Panther," *Chicago Sun Times*, February 28, 2006: 6.

4. Ulysses Blakeley, "Self-Defense Organization (letter to editor)," *Chicago Sun Times*, March 7, 2006: 36; and Ron Grossman and Oscar Avila, "On West Monroe, Hampton's Name Still Resonates," *Chicago Tribune*, March 3, 2006: 1.

5. Gary Washburn, "Hampton Backers May Get Their Way," *Chicago Tribune*, March 30, 2006: 3.

6. Gary Fine, *Difficult Reputations: Collective Memories of the Evil, Inept, and Controversial* (Chicago: University of Chicago Press, 2001).

7. See, for instance, Fath Davis Ruffins, "Mythos, Memory, and History: African American Preservation Efforts, 1820–1990," in Ivan Karp, Christine M. Kreamer,

and Stephen D. Lavine, eds. *Musuems and Communities: The Politics of Public Culture* (Washington, D.C.: Smithsonian Institution Press, 1992), 506–611.

8. The role of Alabama in commemorating the Movement is discussed more fully in Owen J. Dwyer, "Memory on the Margins: Mapping Civil Rights Memorial Landscapes," in Stephen Hanna and Vincent Del Casino, eds., *Mapping Tourism Spaces* (Minneapolis: University of Minnesota Press, 2003), 28–50.

9. "Behind the Scenes," *Birmingham News*, November 15, 1992: special section, 26–27.

10. Bill Osinski, "The Many Signs of MLK," *Atlanta Journal and Constitution*, January 17, 1999: A1.

11. Neil Smith, "Homeless/Global: Scaling Places," in Jon Bird, Barry Curtis, Tim Putnam, George Robertson, and Lisa Tickner, eds., *Mapping the Future: Local Culture, Global Change* (London: Routledge, 1993), 87–119. A critical introduction to scale can be found in Andrew Herod, "Scale: The Local and Global," in Sarah Holloway, Stephen Rice, and Gill Valentine, eds., *Key Concepts in Geography* (London: Sage, 2003), 229–47.

12. Roger W. Stump, "Toponymic Commemoration of National Figures: The Cases of Kennedy and King," *Names* 36 (1988), No. 3/4: 203–16.

13. "Whites in Burke County Win Fight Over Renaming Road," *Atlanta Constitution*, January 13, 1989: A18.

14. Rick Badle, "Gainesville Weighs MLK Road Name," *Atlanta Constitution*, April 20, 2000: 4JJ; and Rick Badle, "Street in Gainesville Renamed for MLK Jr.," *Atlanta Constitution*, May 3, 2000: 4B.

15. Rick Badle, "Gainesville MLK Decision Energizing; Black Leaders Raise Other Issues," *Atlanta Constitution*, May 11, 2000: 4JJ.

16. Peggy Peterman, "What Has Become of the Dream of Naming a Street for Dr. King? (commentary)," *St. Petersburg Times*, May 23, 1987: 1D.

17. Craig Pittman, "King's Fight Still in the Streets: Re-naming of Roads Incites Controversy," *St. Petersburg Times*, April 23, 1990: 1B; and Rick Barry, "King Street, North, South, One Name Only," *Tampa Tribune*, January 19, 2003: Pinellas section, 1.

18. Judy Hill, "Combo Street Name Doesn't Honor King," *Tampa Tribune*, January 14,

2003: Baylife section, 1.

19. Bryan Gilmer, "Symbol of Diversity; Street of Dreams," *St. Petersburg Times*, January 16, 2003: 1B.

20. Doug Wilson, "King Sign Compromise Reached," *Quincy Herald Whig* (online), July 9, 2005: n.p. Last accessed July 2005 at www.whig.com.

21. Kevin McDermott, "Quincy, Ill., Haggles Over a Street for King," *St. Louis Post-Dispatch*, July 4, 2005: A1.

22. Michael McBride, "Longtime Muncie Fixture to End its Run," *The Star Press*, October 21, 2004: 1A.

23. Michael Booth, "Businesses Adjust to Address Change," *Oregon Daily Emerald*, July 8, 2004: 12.

24. Jay Pitts, "Street Renaming Stirs Worry," *St. Petersburg Times*, March 7, 1990: 3B.

25. Craig Pittman, "Mountain of Mail Opposes Street Name Change," *Clearwater Times*, May 28, 1990: 3B.

26. Clarence Page, "Sad Turns but Still Hope for King's Legacy," *Houston Chronicle*, January 15, 1998: 28.

27. Jonathan Tilove, *Along Martin Luther King: Travels on Black America's Main Street* (New York: Random House, 2003), 5–6.

28. Ibid., 17.

29. Matthew Mitchelson, "The Economic Geography of MLK Streets" (unpublished master's thesis: East Carolina University, 2005), 108. For a systematic analysis of economic development along the nation's King streets, see Matthew Mitchelson, Derek H. Alderman, and Jeff Popke, "Branded: The Economic Geographies of MLK Streets," *Social Science Quarterly* 88 (2007), No. 1: 120–45.

30. Portland Development Commission, *IMAGINE a Great Street: N.E. Martin Luther King Jr. Blvd. Transportation Project* (1998), available online at http://www.pD.C.. us/pdf/ura/inner_ne/mlk/smMLKreport.pdf.

31. Sheryll Cashin, "Bucking the Trend: Racially Integrated Communities and Racial Integration," in her book, *The Failures of Integration: How Race and Class are Undermining the American Dream* (New York: Public Affairs, 2004), 39–82.

32. Tilove, op. cit., 164–65.

33. Doug Gross, "Black Leaders Angry Over Statesboro Street Name Law," *Savannah Morning News*, May 22, 1997: 1A.

34. Luke Martin, "City Approves Martin Luther King Jr. Drive," *Statesboro Herald*, December 5, 2002: 1A.

35. Andrew Skerritt, "An Extreme Stance on Street Names," *Pasco Times*, December 16, 2005: 1; and Nicola White, "Renaming Rules Approved," *Tampa Tribune*, January 10, 2006: Pasco section, 1.

36. Jeffrey S. Hampton, "MLK Signs to be Unveiled Though Dispute Goes On," *The Virginian-Pilot*, January 16, 2002: B1.

37. Kirk Beldon Jackson, "Allentown to Evict 'Tent City' Residents," *The Morning Call* (online), February 13, 2005: n.p. Last accessed February 2005 at www.mcall.com; and "News in Brief from Eastern Pennsylvania," *Associated Press State & Local Wire*, February 22, 2005: n.p.

38. T. Scott Batchelor, "West Greenville Group Works to Reshape Redevelopment," *The Daily Reflector*, July 17, 2005: B1.

39. Jim Harger, "MLK Street Names Gets a New Try," *Grand Rapids Press*, June 2, 2004: B1.

40. Jim Harger, "King Street Signs Go Up Monday after Long Fight," *Grand Rapids Press*, March 5, 2005: A1.

41. Jim Harger, "Radio Host is Hopeful in King Dispute," *Grand Rapids Press*, July 13, 2004: A1.

42. Katherine Corcoran, "King Road Renaming Pits Blacks vs. Latinos," *San Jose Mercury News*, October 23, 2003: 1A; and Katherine Corcoran, "King Road Renaming Abandoned," *San Jose Mercury News*, November 5, 2003: 1A.

43. Pat Wilcox, "Unity Asked in Street Name Change," *Chattanooga Times*, March 3, 1981: B1.

44. For a fuller exploration of the Eatonton case, see Derek H. Alderman, "Street Names and the Scaling of Memory: The Politics of Commemorating Martin Luther King, Jr. within the African-American Community," *Area* 35 (2003), No. 2: 163–73.

45. For example, see Gerald R. Webster and Jonathan I. Leib, "Political Culture, Religion, and the Confederate Battle Flag in Alabama, *Journal of Cultural Geography*

20 (2002), No. 1: 1–26; and Edward H. Sebesta and Euan Hague, "The U.S. Civil War as a Theological War: Confederate Christian Nationalism and the League of the South," *Canadian Review of American Studies* 32 (2002), No. 3: 253–84.

46. Quoted in Jeffrey Gettleman, "To Mayor, It's Selma's Statue of Limitation: City's Segregationist Ways Quickly Test First Black to Win Post," *Los Angeles Times*, October 22, 2000: A1.

47. Ibid.

48. Foote, op. cit. The idea of symbolic accretion is developed further in the context of Selma in Owen J. Dwyer, "Symbolic Accretion and Commemoration," *Social and Cultural Geography* 5 (2004): 419–35.

49. See James E. Young, *The Texture of Memory: Holocaust Memorials and Meaning* (New Haven: Yale University Press, 1993); and James E. Young, *At Memory's Edge: After-Images of the Holocaust in Contemporary Art and Architecture* (New Haven: Yale University Press, 2000).

Conclusion

1. Harold E. Gulley, "Women and the Lost Cause: Preserving a Confederate Identity in the American Deep South," *Journal of Historical Geography* 19 (1993), No.2: 125–41; John P. Radford, "Identity and Tradition in the Post-Civil War South," *Journal of Historical Geography* 18 (1992), No. 1: 91–103; and John J. Winberry, "Lest We Forget: The Confederate Monument and the Southern Townscape," *Southeastern Geographer 23* (1983), No. 2: 107–21.

2. Peirce F. Lewis, *New Orleans: The Making of an Urban Landscape, Third Edition*, (Chicago: Center for American Places at Columbia College Chicago, 2008). See, also, Peirce F. Lewis, "Axioms for Reading the Landscape: Some Guides to the American Scene," in Donald W. Meinig, ed., *The Interpretation of Ordinary Landscapes* (New York: Oxford University Press, 1979), 11–32; Peirce F. Lewis, "Learning from Looking: Geographic and Other Writing about the American Cultural Landscape," *American Quarterly* 35 (1983): 242–61; Peirce F. Lewis, "Beyond Description," *Annals of the Association of American Geographers*, 75 (1985),

No. 4: 465–78; Peirce F. Lewis, "Common Landscapes as Historic Documents," in Steven Lubar and W. David Kingery, eds. *History From Things: Essays on Material Culture* (Washington, D.C.: Smithsonian Institute Press, 1993), 115–39; and Peirce F. Lewis, "The Monument and the Bungalow," *Geographical Review* 88 (1998), No. 4: 507–27.

3. Lewis (1979), op. cit., 12.

4. Ibid., 15.

5. The intricacies of geographic field work are discussed at length in a special double issue of *Geographical Review* (2001), edited by Paul Starrs and Dydia DeLyser. Field work in the service of cultural geography is the subject of two edited volumes: Pamela Shurmer-Smith, *Doing Cultural Geography* (London: Sage, 2002); and Alison Blunt et al., *Cultural Geography in Practice* (London: Edward Arnold, 2003). See, also, John C. Hudson, ed., *A Love of the Land: Selected Writings of John Fraser Hart* (Chicago: Center for American Places at Columbia College Chicago, 2008).

6. Lewis would be the first to acknowledge his intellectual debt to the work of other geographers and landscape scholars, including J. B. Jackson and Carl O. Sauer. See, for example, John B. Jackson, "In Search of the Proto-Landscape," in George F. Thompson, ed., *Landscape in America* (Austin: University of Texas Press, 1995), 43–50.

7. Denis E. Cosgrove, *Social Formation and Symbolic Landscape* (Totowa, New Jersey: Barnes & Nobles Books, 1985); James Duncan and Nancy Duncan, "(Re)Reading the Landscape," *Environment and Planning D: Society and Space* 6 (1998): 117–26; James S. Duncan, *The City as Text: The Politics of Landscape Interpretation in Kandyan Kingdom* (Cambridge: Cambridge University Press, 1990); Peter Jackson, *Maps of Meaning: An Introduction to Cultural Geography* (New York: Routledge Press, 1994); and Don Mitchell, *Cultural Geography: A Critical Introduction* (Malden, Mass.: Blackwell Publishers, 2000).

8. John Paul Jones III and Wolfgang Natter, "Space 'and' Representation," in Stanley Brunn, Anne Buttimer, and Ute Wardenga, eds., *Text and Image: Social Construction of Regional Knowledges* (Leipzig, Germany: Selbstverlag Institut für Länderkunde, 1999), 239–47; and Wolfgang Natter and John Paul Jones III, "Identity, Space, and

Other Uncertainties," in Ulf Strohmayer and Georges Benko, eds., *Space and Social Theory* (London: Blackwell Publishers, 1997), 141–61.

9. Recent scholarship on the idea of reading places is featured in a collection of essays dedicated to Yi-Fu Tuan, the esteemed humanistic geographer. See Paul C. Adams, Steven D. Hoelscher, and Karen E. Till, eds., *Textures of Place: Exploring Humanist Geographies* (Minneapolis: University of Minnesota Press, 2001).

10. This notion of people acting out the expectations of a place—and thereby confirming or challenging accepted versions of what is socially right and proper—is developed in two books by Tim Cresswell: *In Place/Out of Place: Geography, Ideology, and Transgression* (Minneapolis: University of Minnesota Press, 1996); and *Place: A Short Introduction* (Malden, Mass.: Blackwell Publishers, 2004).

Suggested Readings, Recordings, and Films

Civil Rights: Biography

Barnard, Hollinger F., ed. *Outside the Magic Circle: The Autobiography of Virginia Foster Durr* (Simon and Schuster, 1987).

Chestnut, Jr., J. L., and Julia Cass. *Black in Selma: The Uncommon Life of J. L. Chestnut, Jr.* (Farrar, Straus and Giroux, 1990).

Clark, Septima Poinsette, and Cynthia Stokes Brown. *Ready from Within: A First Person Narrative* (Africa World Press, 1990).

Lewis, John, and Michael D'Orso. *Walking with the Wind: A Memoir of the Movement* (Simon and Schuster, 1998).

Moody, Anne. *Coming of Age in Mississippi* (Delta, 2004).

Civil Rights: Field Guides

Alabama Bureau of Tourism and Travel (in Montgomery). *Alabama's Black Heritage: A Tour of Historic Sites* (1997).

Carrier, Jim. *A Traveler's Guide to the Civil Rights Movement* (Harvest Books, 2004).

Cobb, Charles E., Jr. *On the Road to Freedom: A Guided Tour of the Civil Rights Trail* (Algonquin Books, 2008).

Davis, Townsend. *Weary Feet, Rested Souls: A Guided History of the Civil Rights Movement* (Norton, 1999).

"We Shall Overcome": Historic Places of the Civil Rights Movement, A National Register of Historic Places Travel Itinerary. Website produced by the U.S. Department of Interior, National Park Service, U.S. Department of Transportation, the Federal Highway Administration, and the National Conference of State Historic Preservation Officers, <http://www.cr.nps.gov/nr/travel/civilrights/index.htm>.

Civil Rights: History

Arsenault, Raymond. *Freedom Riders: 1961 and the Struggle for Racial Justice* (Oxford University Press, 2006).

Branch, Taylor. *Parting the Waters: America in the King Years, 1954–63* (Simon and Schuster, 1988).

———. *Pillar of Fire: America in the King Years, 1963–65* (Simon and Schuster, 1998).

———. *At Canaan's Edge: America in the King Years, 1965–68* (Simon and Schuster, 2006).

Carson, Clayborne. *In Struggle: SNCC and the Black Awakening of the 1960s* (Harvard University Press, 1995).

Carson, Clayborne, and Kris Shepard, eds. *A Call to Consciousness: The Landmark Speeches of Dr. Martin Luther King, Jr.* (New York: IPM/Warner Books, 2001). See, also, http://www.standford.edu/group/king/publications/speeches/contents.htm.

Crawford, Vicki L., Jacqueline Anne Rouse, and Barbara Woods, eds. *Women in the Civil Rights Movement: Trailblazers and Torchbearers, 1941–1965* (Indiana University Press, 1993).

Eskew, Glenn. *But for Birmingham: The Local and National Movements in the Civil Rights Struggle* (University of North Carolina Press, 1997).

Library of America. *James Baldwin: Collected Essays*, selected by Toni Morrison (Literary Classics of the United States, 1998).

———. *Reporting Civil Rights, Part One: American Journalism 1941–1963*, selected by Clayborne Carson, David J. Garrow, Bill Kovach, and Carol Polsgrove (Literary Classics of the United States, 2003).

———. *Reporting Civil Rights, Part Two: American Journalism 1963–1973*, selected by Clayborne Carson, David J. Garrow, Bill Kovach, and Carol Polsgrove (Literary Classics of the United States, 2003).

———. *African American Odyssey*. Website: http://memory.loc.gov/ammem/aaohtml/exhibit/aointro.html.

Morris, Aldon D. *The Origins of the Civil Rights Movement: Black Communities Organizing for Change* (Free Press, 1984).

Smithsonian Folkways Recordings. *Voices of the Civil Rights Movement: Black American Freedom Songs, 1960-1966*, compiled by Bernice Johnson Reagon (Smithsonian Institute, Center for Folklife Programs and Cultural Studies, 1997).

Tuck, Stephen G.N. *Beyond Atlanta: The Struggle for Racial Equality in Georgia, 1940–1980* (University of Georgia Press, 2001).

Civil Rights: The Politics of Collective Memory

Chafe, William, Raymond Gavins, and Robert Korstad, eds. *Remembering Jim Crow: African Americans Tell About Life in the Segregated South* (New Press, 2001). (The book and sound recording are from the "Behind the Veil Project" of the Center for Documentary Studies at Duke University.)

Brundage, W. Fitzhugh. *The Southern Past: A Clash of Race and Memory* (Harvard University Press, 2005).

Daynes, Gary. *Making Villians, Making Heroes: Joesph R. McCarthy, Martin Luther King, Jr., and the Politics of American Memory* (Garland Publishing, 1997).

Discovery Times Channel. *MLK Boulevard: The Concrete Dream* (Documentary written, directed, and produced by Marco Williams, 2003).

Dyson, Michael Eric. *I May Not Get There With You: The True Martin Luther King, Jr.* (Simon & Schuster, 2001).

Nieves, Angel David, and Leslie M. Alexander, eds. *"We Shall Independent Be": African American Place Making in the United States* (University Press of Colorado, 2008).

Romano, Renee, and Leigh Radford, eds. *The Civil Rights Movement in American Memory* (University of Georgia Press, 2006).

Tilove, Jonathan. *Along Martin Luther King: Travels on Black America's Main Street* (Random House, 2003).

Cultural Geography and Landscape Studies

Barton, Craig Evan, ed. *Sites of Memory: Perspectives on Architecture and Race* (Princeton Architectural Press, 2001).

Cresswell, Tim. *Place: A Short Introduction* (Blackwell, 2004).

Foote, Kenneth. *Shadowed Ground: America's Landscapes of Violence and Tragedy, Second Edition* (University of Texas Press, 2003).

Loewen, James. *Lies Across America: What Our Historic Sites Get Wrong* (The New Press, 2000).

Lowenthal, David. *The Past is a Foreign Country* (Cambridge University Press, 1988).

Massey, Doreen. *For Space* (Sage, 2005).

Meinig, Donald W., ed. *The Interpretation of Ordinary Landscapes* (Oxford University Press, 1979).

Mitchell, Don. *Cultural Geography: A Critical Introduction* (Blackwell, 2000).

Schein, Richard, ed. *Landscape and Race in the United States* (Routledge, 2006).

Tuan, Yi-Fu. *Space and Place: The Perspective of Experience* (University of Minnesota Press, 2000).

Young, James E. *The Texture of Memory: Holocaust Memorials and Meaning* (Yale University Press, 1994).

Acknowledgments

Throughout our research we benefited from the insights and experiences of activists, bureaucrats, and citizens who have done much to commemorate the Movement. We are honored by the trust they have placed in us to tell their stories. They include:

- Bernita Sims and the Black Leadership Roundtable, of High Point, North Carolina
- Melvin McLawhorn , Keith Cooper, and Ozie Hall, of the Pitt County chapter of SCLC in Greenville, North Carolina
- Sally Greene, Bill Thorpe, and Fred Battle, of Chapel Hill, North Carolina
- Bill Hull, of the Chattanooga Regional History Museum
- Barbara Andrews, Leila Boyd, and Beverly Robertson, of the National Civil Rights Museum in Memphis, Tennessee
- Jacqueline Smith, of Memphis, Tennessee
- Abigail Jordan and the African-American Monument Association, of Savannah, Georgia
- Frank Catroppa, Art Frederick, Lucy Lawliss, Troy Lissimore, Dean Rowley, Cheryl Shropshire, and Barbara Tagger, of the National Park Service in Atlanta, Georgia
- Reverend C. T. Vivian, of Atlanta, Georgia
- Emma Greshman, of Keysville, Georgia
- Loretta Scott, of Athens, Georgia
- Ulysses Rice and Fannie Pearl Farley, of Eatonton, Georgia
- Donnie Simmons, Joseph Moseley, and Early Humphries, of Statesboro, Georgia
- Jim Baggett, of the Birmingham Public Library's Department of Archives and Manuscripts
- Joanne Bland, Teresa Carter, and Rose Sanders, of the National Voting Rights Museum in Selma, Alabama
- Jean Martin and Jamie Wallace, of Selma, Alabama

- Lee Warner, of the Alabama Historical Commission, and Frances Smiley, of the Alabama Bureau of Tourism and Travel in Montgomery
- Wayne Coleman, Florence Wilson-Davis, Horace Huntley, Lawrence J. Pijeaux, Jr., and Odessa Woolfolk, of the Birmingham Civil Rights Institute
- Steve Spina, of Zephyrhills, Florida
- Dee Ann Sherwood, Levi Rickert, Robert S., and the Community Relations Commission, of Grand Rapids, Michigan
- Pete Meyers, Sean Eversley-Bradwell, and the MLK Street Renaming Project, of Ithaca, New York
- John Patrick Harty and Jim Spencer, of the Martin Luther King, Jr. Memorial Drive Committee, of Manhattan, Kansas
- Katie Mills and students in her 2001 Social Science Writing class at the University of Southern California

Our colleagues and students at the departments of geography at East Carolina University and Indiana University at Indianapolis provided a dynamic intellectual environment for teaching and researching cultural geography. Three former students, Matthew Mitchelson, Christopher McPhilamy, and William Caleb Parker at East Carolina, were essential to collecting data and mapping the nation's Martin Luther King, Jr. streets. Mitchelson's master's thesis was particularly helpful in explaining the economic dimensions of street-naming. Another former East Carolina student, Preston Mitchell, assisted with fieldwork in Savannah and Statesboro, Georgia, and he provided us with a valuable sounding board for understanding the political complexities of street-renaming. In Indianapolis, Alphonso Atkins, Jr. and Annie Gilbert Coleman offered much-needed encouragement and perspective on an early, unloved draft of this book. Mike Maitzen lent us his valuable experience in all things photographic.

More broadly, this project has benefited from the sage advice and kind support of colleagues spread far beyond our home campuses: Maoz Azaryahu, Tom Bell, Carl Dahlman, Dydia DeLyser, Jim Duncan, Gary Fine, Ken Foote, Liz Gagen, Daniel Good, Fon Gordon, Andrew Herod, Steve Hoelscher, John Paul Jones III, Paul Kingsbury, Jolene Kirschenman, Les Lamon, Peirce F. Lewis, Matt McCourt, Ronald Mitchelson, Karl Raitz, Mitch Rose,

Reuben Rose-Redwood, Rich Schein, Barry Schwartz, Gerald Smith, Catherine Souch, Karin Stanford, Jonathan Tilove, Dell Upton, Camille Wells, Robert Weyeneth, Jim Wheeler, Bobby Wilson, and Dana White. You befriended us, taught us, reviewed drafts, and wrote an endless stream of letters on our behalf. We hope we've made you proud.

This book would not have been possible without the generous financial support of several institutions. The inclusion of so many photographs in this book was made possible by the Graham Foundation for Advanced Studies in the Fine Arts. Collective memory is commonly organized and presented via sculpture and the built environment. Exploring its intricacies requires photographs, which in turn require money for acquisition, development, and reproduction. It is an honor to play a part in the Graham Foundation's mission of promoting a deeper appreciation of art and architecture. Further, we extend heartfelt thanks to our colleagues at East Carolina and Indiana universities who supported this project by making funds available that allowed us time to conduct field work, think, and write. Especially critical were grants from Indiana University's Center on Philanthropy and IU's Humanities Initiative grant program and East Carolina's Research Achievement Award. Finally, our original research into the cultural geography of memory was supported by grants from the Association of American Geographers, National Science Foundation, and Rockefeller Foundation's Humanities Fellowship Program hosted by Emory University's Graduate Institute for the Liberal Arts. The support of these organizations is very special indeed, and for it we give thanks.

Finally, our families—Donna and Tyler Alderman in Greenville; Susan, Fiona, Jack, and Meredith Dwyer in Indianapolis—deserve a full measure of gratitude. When we tripped and stumbled along the path, you patiently picked us up and urged us forward. If we've come out right, it's because of you.

Index

List of Acronyms

BCRI	Birmingham Civil Rights Institute
COINTELPRO	Counter Intelligence Program (of the FBI)
FBI	Federal Bureau of Investigation
KKK	Ku Klux Klan
KNHS	King National Historic Site
NAACP	National Association for the Advancement of Colored People
NCRM	National Civil Rights Museum
NPS	National Park Service
NVRM	National Voting Rights Museum
SCLC	Southern Christian Leadership Conference
SNCC	Student Nonviolent Coordinating Committee
WCC	White Citizens Coalition

Text References

About the Authors

Derek H. Alderman (Ph.D., University of Georgia, 1998) is Associate Professor of Cultural and Historical Geography at East Carolina University in Greenville, North Carolina. The author of more than thirty book chapters, journal articles, and essays, Dr. Alderman is a nationally recognized expert on the politics of naming streets and other public places after Martin Luther King, Jr. He has been widely quoted on this subject by the *BBC Radio News*, *CNN*, *Ebony*, *Los Angeles Times*, *Marketplace*, *New York Times*, NPR's *Morning Edition*, and *USA Today*. He frequently consults with activists and municipal leaders involved in naming struggles, and he has delivered community talks across the nation. Dr. Alderman is a former co-editor of *Southeastern Geographer* and the recipient of several research and teaching awards.

Owen J. Dwyer (Ph.D., University of Kentucky, 2000) is Associate Professor of Geography at Indiana University's Indianapolis campus, where he teaches about cities, cartography, and cultural landscapes. Before arriving in Indianapolis, he was a postdoctoral fellow at Emory University and the University of British Columbia. In the course of his research on the politics of public space and commemoration, he has conducted scores of interviews, solicited hundreds of surveys from visitors, and spent long periods of time studying civil rights memorials in Atlanta, Birmingham, Memphis, Montgomery, Selma, and elsewhere. His dissertation fieldwork was supported by the Rockefeller Foundation as well as a grant from the National Science Foundation, the results of which were selected by Columbia University's Graduate School of Architecture, Planning, and Preservation for inclusion in its biannual Temple Hoyne Buell Colloquium on American Architecture. Since then, he has published research articles and book chapters on the subject and has consulted with civil rights museums about visitors demographics and evaluations.

ABOUT THE BOOK:

Civil Rights Memorials and the Geography of Memory is the tenth volume in the *Center Books on the American South* series, George F. Thompson, series founder and director. The book was issued in an edition of 500 hardcover and 2,000 paperback copies, and it was brought to publication with the generous support of the Graham Foundation for Advanced Studies in the Fine Arts and the Friends of the Center for American Places, for which the publisher is most grateful. The text for *Civil Rights Memorials and the Geography of Memory* was set in Goudy Old Style and Optima. The paper is Chinese Goldeast Matte Book, 128 gsm weight. The book was professionally printed and bound in China. For more information about the Center for American Places at Columbia College Chicago, please see p. 144.

FOR THE CENTER FOR AMERICAN PLACES AT COLUMBIA COLLEGE CHICAGO:

George F. Thompson, Founder and Director

Brandy L. Savarese, Associate Editorial Director

Amber K. Lautigar, Operations Manager and Marketing Coordinator

A. Lenore Lautigar, Associate Editor and Publishing Liaison

Elizabeth S. Dattilio and Sara E. Lovelace, Editorial Assistants

Ashleigh Frank and Purna Makaram, Manuscript Editors

Dawn Hachenski, Book Designer

David Skolkin, Art Director

Dave Keck, of Global Ink Inc., Production Coordinator

Center for American Places

AT COLUMBIA COLLEGE CHICAGO

The Center for American Places at Columbia College Chicago is a nonprofit organization, founded in 1990 by George F. Thompson, whose educational mission is to enhance the public's understanding of, appreciation for, and affection for the places of the Americas and the world—whether urban, suburban, rural, or wild. Underpinning this mission is the belief that books provide an indispensable foundation for comprehending and caring for the places where we live, work, and commune. Books live. Books endure. Books make a difference. Books are gifts to civilization.

Since 1990 the Center for American Places has brought to publication more than 320 books under its imprint and in association with numerous publishing partners. Center books have won or shared more than 100 editorial awards, prizes, and citations, including multiple best-book honors in more than thirty fields of study.

For more information, please send inquiries to the Center for American Places at Columbia College Chicago, 600 South Michigan Avenue, Chicago, Illinois 60605-1996, U.S.A., or visit the Center's Website (www.americanplaces.org).